WILLIAM JAMES ON
THE COURAGE TO BELIEVE

AMERICAN PHILOSOPHY SERIES

WILLIAM JAMES
ON
THE COURAGE
TO BELIEVE

Second Edition

ROBERT J. O'CONNELL, S.J.

FORDHAM UNIVERSITY PRESS
New York
1997

LC 97–12135
ISBN 0–8232–1727–2 (*hardcover*)
ISBN 0–8232–1728–0 (*paperback*)
ISSN 1073–2764
American Philosophy Series No. 8
Vincent M. Colapietro, Editor
Vincent G. Potter (1929–1994), Founding Editor

Library of Congress Cataloging-in-Publication Data

O'Connell, Robert J.
 William James on the courage to believe / Robert J. O'Connell.—
[2nd rev. ed.]
  p.   cm.
Includes bibliographical references and index.
ISBN 0-8232-1727-2. — ISBN 0-8232-1728-0 (pbk.)
1. James, William, 1842–1910. Will to believe.   2. Philosophy.
3. Belief and doubt.   I. Title.
B945.J23W536   1997
121'.6—DC21   97-12135
                                                              CIP

Printed in the United States of America

To
all my exemplars
of the courage to believe
starting with
my sisters
JANE, MARGARET, ELLEN, and MARY
and my brother
JOHN
but going on
and on
and on

Contents

Preface

Two of the three appendix chapters added here to the original text of *William James on the Courage to Believe* have already been published, in the form of articles, substantially as they appear here.

Along with the final chapter, entitled "James's Voluntarism: Readiness, Willingness, or Will to Believe?" they present sharpened treatments of three central axial contentions from the original essay. The importance of these contentions had not, it seemed to me, been sufficiently appreciated even by the friendliest of my critics.

For I still contend, and expand on that contention here, without becoming unrelievedly deontological, that James's ethics does boast a deontological "streak" which saves his "Will to Believe" argument from succumbing to the fatal flaw of "wishful thinking." The presence of that "streak," I go on to contend, both requires and permits a more accurate interrelationship of those four distinct attitudes—right, readiness, willingness, and resolute "will" to believe—as they interweave with and lend each other material support in the course of James's argument. In my closing essay here, finally, previously unpublished, I try to clarify the unique epistemological situation implied in the oddity that, if we understand all the foregoing constituents as James does (when he is thinking "at top form"), then our consent to the "facts" at issue here does not, paradoxically, receive support from the *weltanschaulich* belief proposition. The true state of affairs implies something closer to the opposite: it might turn out to be the legitimate function of a resolute "willing faith" to lend those facts their aura of believability and thereby cement the reciprocal relationships implied in the right, will, willingness, and readiness to believe.

I am happy to express my thanks to *The Transactions of the Charles S. Peirce Society* for permission to reprint "'The Will to Believe' and James's Deontological Streak," and to the *International Philosophical Quarterly* for permission to reprint "Faith and Facts in James's 'Will to Believe.'" I also wish to thank the Fordham University Press, and particularly Mr. Saverio Procario and Dr. Mary Beatrice Schulte, for their generous compliance with my request to unite these newer and older materials into this book.

ACKNOWLEDGMENTS

THANKS for help on this study must go first to those who consented to read it, and who offered a number of valuable comments: to Professors W. Norris Clarke, s.j., and Robert J. Roth, s.j., of Fordham University, who read it in an earlier and briefer version; and to Professors Joseph Grassi of Fairfield University, John Lachs of Vanderbilt University, and John Smith of Yale University, who commented generously on the later and longer version that eventually became this book. My gratitude to them is only the keener in view of the forbearance some of them were constrained to show: I confess to a few seizures of obstinacy which led me to cling to certain views that some of my friendly critics found less congenial than I did. Wherever our differences remain, however, I hope they will credit me with having striven, at least, to ground my case on the evidence of William James's writings.

I owe further debts of gratitude to the authorities of Fordham University who granted me the Faculty Fellowship year that resulted in this work; of Fairfield University, and particularly Rev. Christopher E. Mooney, s.j., Academic Vice President; and of Vanderbilt University, and particularly Dr. Jack Forstman, Dean of the Divinity School, for according me Visiting Scholar privileges and the warmest of hospitality during the time devoted to writing this book.

Last, but far from least, my fond and admiring thanks (once again) to the world's première typist, Mrs. Karen Harris, and to that rare fusion of personal *jucunditas* and editorial *severitas*, Dr. Mary Beatrice Schulte.

ABBREVIATIONS

DD   "The Dilemma of Determinism"
LWL   "Is Life Worth Living?"
MP   "The Moral Philosopher and the Moral Life"
RA   "Reflex Action and Theism"
SR   "The Sentiment of Rationality"
WB   "The Will to Believe"

Although I have profited from the critical edition of these lectures published in the sixth volume of *The Works of William James* (see below), my page references are to the more familiar and commonly used Dover edition (*The Will to Believe and Other Essays in Popular Philosophy* [New York: Dover Publications, 1956]). *Works* 489–90 provides a helpful key to the page correspondences in these two editions.

Letters   *The Letters of William James.* Ed. Henry James. 2 vols. Boston: Atlantic Monthly Press, 1920.

PP   *The Principles of Psychology.* 2 vols. New York: Dover Publications, 1950.

Works   *The Works of William James.* VI. *The Will to Believe and Other Essays in Popular Philosophy.* Edd. Frederick H. Burkhardt, Fredson Bowers, and Ignas K. Skrupselis. Intro. Edward H. Madden. Cambridge: Harvard University Press, 1979.

WILLIAM JAMES ON
THE COURAGE TO BELIEVE

Introduction

IT IS SOMETIMES HARD TO REALIZE that William James's lecture on "The Will to Believe" must actually date from nearly ninety years ago, the spirit animating its every line is so unquenchably youthful; we almost fancy we can hear James delivering it. And its appeal to young philosophical minds seems never to grow old.

For nearly twenty years now, I have used it (along with others) as a text for introductory courses in philosophy, and never cease to marvel at its power. For James himself, when he gave it as a lecture, it represented an occasion to have his "say about the deepest reasons of the universe," and to say that say with the fullest human resources at his command. Youthful minds, more haunted by those cosmic questions than we often give them credit for, and at the same time so responsive to the broad humanity, not merely the braininess, of thinkers who address them, delight in James as in a kindred spirit; they find it hard to believe he ever grew a gray hair.

But professional philosophers of every stamp have equally succumbed to "The Will to Believe." Once read, it does not admit of being easily left aside: it bothers the mind and heart somewhat as Plato's *Symposium*, Augustine's *Confessions*, and Pascal's *Pensées* do. Its provocative power has stimulated adverse criticisms, some of them fierce, as well as equally impassioned essays in defense; it will not let us rest. Philosophers naturally come at an essay of this sort with their own preoccupations, priorities, and methodological suppositions; it is a rare essay, though, that can respond to such a varied lot of thinkers by providing such chewy grist for each of their mills.

My own interest in "The Will to Believe" and its companion lectures was intensified by my having to deal with problems arising from St. Augustine's theory of art. How, for instance, do a thinker's artistic sensibility, and even artistic theory, enter into the personal way he, or she, shapes and addresses larger philosophic issues? And how legitimately do those artistic and aesthetic biases play a role in the activity of philosophizing? Relevant to Augustine, the same question intrudes upon our evaluations of Plato, Nietzsche, Heidegger, Dewey, and, of course, James—to stay with some outstanding instances.

The entryway we take toward studying anyone's philosophy will always influence the conclusions we eventually draw; surely it is partially due to my peculiar entryway that I have come to the conviction that, with some critical honing, "The Will to Believe" still articulates some very substantial and important truths, both for young minds and for older ones. Some of the conclusions I come to here have already been suggested elsewhere; I have, I hope, not missed acknowledging any of the thinkers to whom I am indebted for those suggestions. That James's lecture applies to our "over-beliefs" has been said before, but I have tried to draw out some implications of that view which have not received the recognition they deserve. Chief among those implications is my claim that James is proposing that the "passional" side of our nature intervenes from the very first move we make toward settling on those *weltanschaulich* positions he calls "over-beliefs," and not only from the moment when the intellect's survey of the "evidence" has reached an impasse. This might seem, at first, to convict James once for all of having commended "wishful thinking," a charge so frequently repeated in the literature. My second major claim is that a number of defenses made of James against that "wishful thinking" charge are well-intentioned doubtless, but clearly off-target, since it is not James they end up defending. Can he be defended? My final claim is, yes—but only if we take seriously the deontological side of his moral thought, so often neglected, along with the epistemological corollary of that deontology: that only the thinker of developed moral character can be expected to "see" our universe in appropriate moral terms. Merely an echo of Aristotle's warnings about teaching philosophy to the young, or of Plato's claim that only one sensibilized to beauteous forms can glimpse the Forms? In short, is James dusting off a modern version of the old traditional stress on "knowledge by connaturality"? To some extent. But even if he were (unwittingly) doing no more than that, he does it as only James could: incomparably.

One reason for the variety of criticisms and defenses of "The Will to Believe" is that critics and defenders are not always reading the same lecture, or reading it in the same way. They tend to highlight different moments of the argument, sometimes taking James's contentions out of context when they do so. Beyond that, there are elements in James's argument to which, I shall claim, almost none of them attributes the importance that they held for James himself. Before I can defend what I find defensible in his lecture, accordingly, I am bound in the first place to justify my own reading of it. Hence, my opening chapter: I trace James's argument, pointing up its crucial turnings, its sometimes subtle shifts in logic or meaning of terms, and calling the reader's attention to those features which, more generally ignored or slighted by previous writers, become important for the qualified defense I mean eventually to make of James.

But how seriously did James himself take this lecture? View him as a psychologist on a metaphysical holiday, or take his occasional slips in expression and his general vivacity of spirit as indications of a cavalier or "sporting" attitude toward his topic, and you will read his lecture out of an attitude and set of suppositions that may seriously affect not only your evaluation, but your very understanding of his argument. My second chapter, then, attempts to place this lecture in James's overall philosophical effort, in order to display how seriously he meant it, and how seriously we have a right to take it.

One of the fiercest critics of James's contentions has gotten considerable mileage out of viewing his lecture through the lens provided by the famous Wager argument from Blaise Pascal's *Pensées*: the view John Hick takes of Pascal, and the attitude he assumes James had to Pascal's Wager, color his entire criticism. Hence, the need for a closer examination of James's relationship to Pascal; I undertake that in Chapter 3.

But the central conclusion of Hick's criticism comes down to a recent version of the objection that has dogged James's proposals since they first saw the light of day: that he was providing mankind with neither more nor less than a reckless license for "wishful thinking." Chapter 4 examines both the grounds that have been offered for that objection and the varied strategies that a number of James's defenders have adopted in answering it.

Both critics and defenders, however, share a number of assumptions about how James's central thesis should be understood. They regularly suppose that the validity of his contentions can be tested by application to "outcome" cases; Chapter 5 examines that assumption, and strives to show that the thesis of "The Will to Believe" legitimately applies only to what James called over-beliefs, or propositions of *weltanschaulich* dimensions.

Building on that conclusion, Chapter 6 advances what will strike many readers as the most outrageous contention in this study: that, contrary to what has been almost universally supposed, James did not mean to affirm that our passional nature should intervene in the formation of our over-beliefs only *after* our dispassionate intellects have failed to resolve the issues one way or the other. The surprising fact of the matter is that, early and late, James (like Pascal!) consistently taught that the passional or volitional side *de facto* exercises a precursive influence on all such intellectual surveys, and that it would be idly asking for the psychologically impossible to insist on the reverse scenario. James clearly held that the "will" to believe exerts its influence before, during, and after the formation of our over-beliefs, directing, influencing, and virtually commanding all such surveys, whether we admit it or no.

This surprising thesis seems to throw us back into an even stronger version of "wishful thinking." Are the beliefs we come to adopt simply the pre-ordained products of our individual temperaments? Or is there more to the passional side of our nature than wish, temperament, preference, and the like? Chapter 7 investigates what James has written about the various strata of the passional, and suggests ways in which his central thesis can be salvaged from the shipwreck of epistemological irresponsibility. Chapter 8 confirms and expands those findings by exploring the various metaphors James employed in his discussions of belief.

An Epilogue briefly indicates why James's positions, if understood as I have interpreted them, remain valid reformulations of a long-standing and quite honorable view of what philosophical thinking is truly about—reformulations which, I submit, signpost some escape routes out of the impasse in which the philosophical profession, and the business of philosophical education, find themselves mired at present.

1

The Argument
of
"The Will to Believe"

"THE WILL TO BELIEVE" is one of a series of "popular" lectures in philosophy to which James devoted much of his time between the years 1880 and 1896. At the height of his fame, and in need of supplemental income for the education of his children, he was also much sought-after as a lecturer. His audience in this case was the membership of the Philosophy Clubs of Yale and Brown universities, in the year 1896.

Beginning on a light note, he portrays himself as about to deliver "something like a sermon" on "justification," not "by," but "*of*," faith (WB 1); at least it will assure them that such matters are still spoken about in their sister-university Harvard! James then states his aim more precisely: he hopes to present "a defence of our right to adopt a believing attitude in religious matters, in spite of the fact that our merely logical intellect may not have been coerced. 'The Will to Believe,' accordingly, is the title of my paper" (WB 1–2). In the months and years to follow, James will have second thoughts on that nonchalant "accordingly": the "right" to believe may be one thing, but the "will" to believe quite a different matter.[1]

His main contention, however, is stated further on in greater detail:

> Our passional nature[2] not only lawfully may, but must, decide an option between propositions, whenever it is a genuine option that cannot by its nature be decided on intellectual

grounds; for to say, under such circumstances, "Do not decide, but leave the question open," is itself a passional decision,— just like deciding yes or no,—and is attended with the same risk of losing the truth [WB 11].

That statement of his "thesis" supposes several semi-technical distinctions he has begun with. An option, for James, involves a "decision between two hypotheses," but a "genuine" option must possess three characteristics: it must be "forced," "living," and "momentous." A "living option," the first kind James explains, is one in which both competing hypotheses are "live" ones; that is, they both exert an "appeal" as real possibilities to the mind of the person weighing them (WB 2). He assumes, in illustrating this property, that the advice to become a Mohammedan, a theosophist, or a believer in the Mahdi would exert no such appeal to the students of Yale and Brown, so that the question of deciding for one rather than the other would be a "dead" option—if not for an Arab or African—at least for them.[3] Not so, however, the option between Christianity and agnosticism, for in this case, "trained as you are, each hypothesis makes some appeal, however small, to your belief" (WB 3).

But a genuine option must also be "momentous" rather than "trivial." An invitation to reach for the kind of immortality involved in joining Nansen's North Pole expedition, for example, would represent a "momentous" option, a unique opportunity, in which the stakes are significant and the decision irreversible. "He who refuses to embrace a unique opportunity loses the prize as surely as if he tried and failed" (WB 4).[4]

The third characteristic of a genuine option is that it be "forced": the two possibilities presented form a "complete logical disjunction"—" 'Either accept this truth or go without it' "—with "no standing place outside of the alternative," and "no possibility of *not* choosing" (WB 3; emphasis added for clarity) between them.

It would seem, at the outset, that the option James is about to discuss—"Either believe in God, or do not believe"—has already been ruled out as a "genuine" option: for a third possibility, that of remaining essentially indifferent to the question, and acquiescing in an agnosticism which is neither belief nor disbelief, seems to offer a "standing ground" outside of these two contending possibilities. It will be part of James's task further on to argue that this third possibility is, in the last analysis, illusory; but we shall come to that in time.

One would expect as James's next move that he explain that crucial term in his "thesis": our "passional" or "volitional nature." Instead, he rather too easily supposes his auditors' familiarity with what he means, and passes on to illustrate that meaning. There are, he admits, cases where it seems "preposterous" to talk of "our opinions being modifiable at will" (WB 4): we cannot, however strongly we will it, deny the existence of Abraham Lincoln or the reality of a rheumatic attack: such Humean "matters of fact . . . and relations between ideas" are "either there or not there for us" and "if not there cannot be put there by any action of our own" (WB 5). Any talk of our believing in such propositions because we will to believe in them is nothing less than "silly" (WB 7).

As another provisional objection to his own thesis, James reminds his hearers of Pascal's famous Wager argument. Grossly put: bet on God's existence and, if He does exist, you win eternal happiness; if He does not exist, life being so short, what have you lost? James proceeds to summarize the Wager in his own fashion. That summary I shall have to deal with further on; what is interesting at this point is James's dismissal of the Wager. For dismiss it he does, and on two distinct grounds.[5] First, "when religious faith expresses itself thus, in the language of the gaming-table," one is entitled to feel it has been "put to its last trumps"; a faith adopted "after such a mechanical calculation would lack the inner soul of faith's reality"—and we, in the Deity's place, would "probably take particular pleasure in cutting off believers of this pattern from their infinite reward" (WB 6). Betting on God's existence by calculating the gains and losses respectively entailed by belief and unbelief, James is clearly suggesting, is an entirely unworthy approach to religious faith.[6]

The second flaw in Pascal's argument, as James views it, and assumes his auditors all view it as he does, is that faith "in masses and holy water" represents a "dead" option, a set of "foregone impossibilities" to "us Protestants." So, says James in a remarkable parallel, would an invitation tendered by the Mahdi to wager on *him* as the guarantee of our eternal happiness! The Mahdi's logic would be the same as Pascal's, James observes, but the "hypothesis he offers us is dead," as dead as the one offered by Pascal.

May one seriously talk, then, of "believing by our volition"? Catering still to his auditors' suspicion of all such talk, James permits himself a rhetorical flight evoking the "magnificent edifice of the physical sciences," the construction of so many "disinterested moral lives" over the centuries: how utterly "besotted and contemptible" seems any sentimentalist who would ignore such scientific findings and "decide things from out of his private dream." One can understand why scientific thinkers, bred in this "rugged and manly school" should feel like "spewing such subjectivism out of their mouths" (WB 7). One can understand, as well, why some such thinkers, in their antipathy to subjectivism and sentimentalism, "pass over to the opposite extreme entirely"; Clough, Huxley, and W. K. Clifford—James's principal adversary[7]—close ranks in preaching the immorality, desecration, and downright sinfulness involved in *anyone's* believing *anything* " 'on insufficient evidence,' " no matter how strongly that belief might work toward the " 'solace and private pleasure of the believer' " (WB 8). The scientific conscience, then, would seem to anathematize the very possibility James is about to argue for: that "wish and will and sentimental preference" —factors of our passional or volitional nature—may rightly intervene in the formation of beliefs of any sort whatever.

But, interposes James, however healthy Clifford's ethics of belief may sound, he is flying in the face of facts; for it is a fact that we believe a host of things—from molecular theory to Protestant Christianity—not from any personal insight into evidence, but swayed by the authority and prestige those beliefs have acquired in our particular "intellectual climate" (WB 9).[8] And it is another fact that even the Cliffords of the scientific world disbelieve a whole array of facts and theories on the passional, rather than "logical," grounds that they have no "use" for those facts and theories; indeed, Clifford's very "law" that we should rule out our "willing nature" in the formation of our beliefs is itself based on his "wish" to exclude all views and theories for which he, in his professional capacity, can find no use!

The factual state of things, therefore, is far less simple than Clifford would allow: it is true, even for him, that our "non-intellectual nature does influence our convictions. . . . and pure insight and logic, whatever they might do ideally, are not the only things that really do produce our creeds" (WB 11). But all this serves only to sharpen the question: Is this intervention of our volitional nature "reprehensible and pathological," or, on the contrary, a "normal element in making up our minds"? We have already seen James's programatic answer to that question, in the "thesis" transcribed above; now, too, we are in a better position to appreciate how circumscribed an answer it purports to be. This much, at least, is indisputably clear. James is not claiming that the intervention of our passional nature is legitimate in any and every option we may be faced with. His claim is the much more limited one that volitional intervention is legitimate where the option in question is

"genuine"—is living, forced, and momentous. Three necessary conditions, but are they sufficent conditions as well?
James's expression is tantalizing: *"whenever it is a genuine
option that cannot by its nature be decided on intellectual
grounds."* The italics are James's own; obviously, the qualification was important to him. And yet nothing in the
discussion so far has gone to clarify exactly what he intends
by it. But we shall come to see that such clarity is indispensable if we are to gauge the value of his argument.

Having stated his thesis, James sees the need of clearing
up two more "preliminary" points before endeavoring to
argue it. The first has to do with the human tendency to be
"absolutist" and "dogmatic" in epistemological matters:
to claim that our feeling of certainty is validated by our
possessing the "objective evidence" that grounds our certainty. And yet, how many positions down the history of
philosophy have made that claim, against adversaries who
made the identical claim for their perfectly antithetical
views! The only solution to this impasse, James proposes,
is to abandon the "absolutist" mentality once for all, to
admit, like a true empiricist, that each of our views is rein-
terpretable and corrigible. Giving up the absolutist doctrine of "objective certitude," however, is not the same as
giving up "the quest or hope of truth itself" (WB 17); it
means that the empiricist, as James ideally sees him, com-
mits himself to the task of "systematically continuing to
roll up experiences and think," and in that thinking, to
face future-ward rather than toward the past, toward the
"outcome, the upshot," the *terminus ad quem* rather than
the origin and *terminus a quo* of his thinking. Of any of
his hypotheses, the Jamesian empiricist must ask, not how
it came to him, but whether "the total drift of thinking continues to confirm it."

The second "preliminary": there are two ways, James
asserts, of formulating our epistemological rule of conduct.
We may say *"We must know the truth"*; or we may say

"we must avoid error." Often jumbled together as though
they were two ways of stating the same epistemological
commandment, these are, in fact, "two separable laws."
Clifford, for example, when legislating against belief without sufficient evidence, has made the avoidance of error his
primary concern; but in doing so, he is merely expressing
his fear—his *passional* fear—of being duped; that fear he
has allowed to dominate his desire for attaining truth,
making that desire a secondary concern. But what if one
chooses—and that choice *is* a choice, dictated as much by
the passional as Clifford's choice in the opposing direction
—what if one chooses to make the "chase for truth" (WB
18) a paramount, and the avoidance of error a secondary,
concern? To an empiricist philosopher, Clifford sounds too
much like a general nervously exhorting his troops to keep
clear of the battle rather than risk a single wound. Obviously, James is confident that his audience by this time will
concede him the right to make the search for truth his paramount concern, with the understanding that his preference
for that epistemological canon is at least as legitimate as
Clifford's choice of the opposing one. And that concession
frees him, at last, to go straight to the main question of his
lecture.

He first refreshes his hearers on the limited application
of his main thesis. The "attitude of sceptical balance" and
its concomitant decision to wait for further evidence are
often the appropriate one—in scientific matters, for example; but the judgments we are called upon to make about
such disputed questions as Roentgen's theory or the causal-
ity of conscious states are seldom if ever either forced or
momentous.[9] They are not, therefore, the kind of genuine
option to which James's thesis applies. But are there not,
among our speculative questions, examples of "forced options" which do not permit us to "wait with impunity till
the coercive evidence shall have arrived" (WB 22)?[10]

James proposes two areas where such options confront

us; the first of them is the realm of moral beliefs: here we must consult, not science, but what Pascal calls the "heart," for it is a question, not of what sensibly exists, but of what is "good," what solicits our "moral preferences"—what appeals to the will. "If your heart does not *want* a world of moral reality, your head will assuredly never make you believe in one," and when we choose to "stick to it" that there is such a thing as moral truth, "we do so with our whole nature," not merely with our pure intellects (WB 23).

But there is a second realm where the same thing applies: this realm is concerned with "facts," but those peculiar facts involved in "personal relations, states of mind between one man and another." Whether another person likes me or not will most often depend on "whether I meet you half-way, am willing to assume that you must like me, and show you trust and expectation." That "previous faith" on my part is what so often "makes your liking come" (WB 23–24). But if I stand aloof and wait for "objective evidence" that you do like me, then "ten to one your liking never comes" (WB 24).

At this juncture, James's argument has taken a subtle shift: instead of staying with the question whether, as a matter of *fact*, "you like me or not," he has veered round to recommending the show of "trust and expectation," a "previous faith" that you will *come* to like me, as the most effective way of making that liking "come." Continuing on that same tack, he observes that the "desire for a certain kind of truth here brings about that special truth's existence," not only in friendships, but in the quest for "promotions, boons, appointments," in "innumerable cases of other sorts." The faith of the ambitious and confident young executive, for instance, "acts on the powers above him like a claim, and creates its own verification."

The same rule holds, James continues, for any social

organism. A team, college, government, or army all depend on each member's doing his job with the "precursive faith" that the others will do their job as well; without this, "not only is nothing achieved, but nothing is even attempted."

> A whole train of passengers (individually brave enough) will be looted by a few highwaymen, simply because the latter can count on one another, while each passenger fears that if he makes a movement of resistance, he will be shot before any one else backs him up. If we believed that the whole car-full would rise at once with us, we should each severally rise, and train-robbing would never even be attempted [WB 24–25].

There are, then, cases "where a fact cannot come at all unless a preliminary faith exists in its coming" (WB 25). So, James concludes emphatically, "*where faith in a fact can help create the fact*, that would be an insane logic which should say that faith running ahead of scientific evidence is the 'lowest kind of immorality.' . . . Yet such is the logic by which our scientific absolutists pretend to regulate our lives!"[11]

Now James passes on from "human cases" to the more cosmic question represented by the "religious hypothesis." Since religions "differ so much in their accidents," James feels obliged to express the religious hypothesis in "very generic and broad" terms. "Religion" says, first, that "the best things are the more eternal things," that " 'Perfection is eternal' "; and, secondly, that "we are better off even now if we believe her first affirmation to be true" (WB 26). James supposes his auditors will grant it as a "living" hypothesis, at least, that *both* these affirmations may be true. But then, it is evident that religion offers itself as a "momentous" option as well: belief and unbelief will issue, respectively, in gain and loss of a "certain vital good."

That "vital good" is left unexplained in this essay; but since James is about to revert to the idiom of the "gaming-table," it is worth observing that the terms of his wager are quite different from Pascal's. James says nothing about the "eternal" happiness to be won; he does not exclude it, surely, but the "vital good" he is invoking seems clearly a good to be gained "even now," in this human life before death and whatever may follow on death.[12]

How much that undefined, unexplained "vital good" must have appealed to the students of Brown and Yale is anyone's guess, of course; its vacuity as it stands, though, must have been underlined by the lofty generality of James's definition of "religion." True, he felt that a "generic and broad" characterization was forced upon him by the needs of his argument; but one cannot help hearing Pascal himself, whispering behind the scenes about that antiseptic, bloodless being, the "God of the philosophers." A "momentous" hypothesis, really? But a lecture is a lecture, and one has only a certain amount of time. We must not fault him overmuch if, with other fish to fry, James hurtles onward.

For he sees his thorniest task as that of showing that the religious option is truly "forced." After all, "belief" and "unbelief" do not seem to represent two terms of a perfect logical disjunction; between them would appear to lie that middle "standing-ground," "non-belief": the uncommitted position of "remaining sceptical and waiting for more light," until " 'sufficient evidence' for religion be found" (WB 27). But that appearance, James argues, is illusory: take a man who hesitates to marry, unsure whether his wife-to-be will turn out to be an angel when he brings her home; when it comes to gaining or losing that particular "angel-possibility," is there any real difference between his hesitating indefinitely and never marrying at all, or deciding to marry someone else instead of that possible angel? No, argues James; he "cut[s] himself off from that particular angel-possibility" (WB 26) as decisively in one case as in the other. The indefinite postponement of decision is, to be sure, a way of "avoiding error," on the supposition that the religious hypothesis is untrue; but *if it is true,* "we lose the good" it puts before us "just as certainly as if we positively chose to disbelieve." The skeptical choice of waiting for conclusive evidence, then, is itself a kind of *positive* option, as much fraught with risk as the options to believe or disbelieve: the skeptic is "actively playing his stake as much as the believer is; he is backing the field against the religious hypothesis, just as the believer is backing the religious hypothesis against the field."

The Pascalian Wager language may not be that "silly," when all is said: in any event, James's ambiguity toward Pascal's maneuver has become more baffling than ever. But now he probes more searchingly into the motivation of the skeptic: instead of the cool-headed, passionless abstention skepticism would claim to be, in reality it would strive to persuade us that, when it comes to the religious hypothesis, "to yield to our fear of its being error is wiser and better than to yield to our hope that it may be true" (WB 27). The skeptic is not preaching "intellect against passions," then; he is preaching "fear" against "hope"—"intellect with one passion laying down its law." But what entitles "fear" to the palm of "supreme wisdom" in these matters? "Dupery for dupery, what proof is there that dupery through hope is so much worse than dupery through fear?"

The "scientist," then, is not dissuading me from choosing an option; he is trying to persuade me to choose "his kind of option." In a situation where "my own stake is important enough to give me the right to choose my own form of risk," he is commanding me to "forfeit my sole chance in life of getting on the winning side."

But all this supposes, of course, that I am willing "to run the risk of acting as if my passional need of taking the world religiously might be prophetic and right," and, what is more, that it may, indeed, be "prophetic and right," in such wise that religion be a "live hypothesis which may be true."

Is it far-fetched to think that James is betraying, here, an uneasiness about his preceding definition of "religion"—a definition so "generic and broad" as to drain it of all the juices that should flow through a truly "momentous" hypothesis? However that may be, he does evoke for his hearers the "further way" in which religion "comes to most" of them. One might object that James is about to present not merely a "further," but a more particular, even an accidental, form of the religious hypothesis he first felt it necessary to keep "generic and broad"; but that might be caviling. The "perfect and . . . eternal" in the universe, he now admits, is "represented in our religions as having personal form," so that if we are religious, the universe becomes "no longer a mere *It* to us, but a *Thou*." This puts James in position to exploit his foregoing observations on "person to person" relationships. He recasts them in a fresh illustration:

> just as a man who in a company of gentlemen made no advances, asked a warrant for every concession, and believed no one's word without proof, would cut himself off by such churlishness from all the social rewards that a more trusting spirit would earn,—so here, one who should shut himself up in snarling logicality and try to make the gods extort his recognition willy-nilly, or not get it at all, might cut himself off forever from his only opportunity of making the gods' acquaintance [WB 28].

So, James is arguing, if we entertain the notion that the "perfect and . . . eternal" is personal, thus making the universe a "Thou," it should come as no surprise that "We feel . . . as if the appeal of religion to us were made to our own active good-will, as if evidence might be forever withheld from us unless we met the hypothesis half-way": very much the way, in his earlier illustration from the interpersonal sphere, James argued for the "half-way" meeting between two who would be friends.

Now, however, he takes another step; the unbroken sweep of his prose would imply that it follows easily from what has gone before, if not for our minds, then at least for his:

> This feeling, forced on us we know not whence, that by obstinately believing that there are gods . . . we are doing the universe the deepest service we can, seems part of the living essence of the religious hypothesis. If the hypothesis *were* true in all its parts, including this one, then pure intellectualism, with its veto on our making willing advances, would be an absurdity; and some participation of our sympathetic nature would be logically required.

The "logic" appealed to here is the logic of interpersonal relationships; so much for the continuity presiding over James's argument in this paragraph. But a new, even a solemn, note has been injected; it is no longer merely a matter of gaining the rewards of friendship. The essence of the "religious" hypothesis has for one incandescent moment been acknowledged in different terms: in terms of "doing the universe the deepest service we can."

This said, James feels, he has made it clear why he cannot accept such "agnostic rules" as Clifford and others would impose, rules that would "keep [our] willing nature out of the game." His final formulation runs: "I cannot do so for this plain reason, that *a rule of thinking which would absolutely prevent me from acknowledging certain kinds of truth if those kinds of truth were really there, would be an irrational rule.* That for me is the long and short of the formal logic of the situation . . . [WB 28–29]."

James closes in a frankly hortatory vein, by quoting from Fitzjames Stephen. We all must deal with the " 'riddles of the Sphinx' " encased in such questions as " 'What do you think of yourself?' " and " 'What do you think of the world?' " and " 'choice' " is involved in whatever way we deal with them. " 'In all important transactions of life,' " Stephen points out, "we have to take a leap in the dark. . . . We stand on a mountain pass in the midst of whirling snow and blinding mist, through which we get glimpses now and then of paths which may be deceptive. If we stand still we shall be frozen to death. If we take the wrong road we shall be dashed to pieces. We do not certainly know whether there is any right one. What must we do? 'Be strong and of a good courage.' Act for the best, hope for the best, and take what comes. . . . If death ends all, we cannot meet death better" [WB 30–31].

These are James's final injunctions. He was fond of this metaphor of the Alpinist's quandary;[13] it regularly evoked, for him, the notion of "courage," the courage he thought of as energizing the "will" to take the leap of faith. The force of these closing remarks we shall explore more carefully as this evaluation of his lecture comes, in its own turn, to a close.

NOTES

1. In fact, ensuing discussion of his lecture will crystallize into a scholarly consensus which James seems to have anticipated, and sympathetically: that he argued successfully for a *right*, but not for a *will*, to believe. See the evidence and argument presented by Gail Kennedy in "Pragmatism, Pragmaticism, and the Will to Believe— A Reconsideration," *The Journal of Philosophy*, 55, No. 14 (July 3, 1958), 578–88. For my own refinements on this proposal, see below, chap. 6.

2. By our "passional nature" James refers to that part, side, or (in the terms applied in RA, passim) "willing department" of our total human nature which interacts with our "perceiving" and "conceiving" departments. See WB 29–30 where "heart, instincts, and courage," "senses," and "intellect" clearly designate those same three departments, though in different terms. Patrick K. Dooley, in "The Nature of Belief: The Proper Context for James' 'The Will to Believe,' " *Transactions of the Charles S. Peirce Society*, 8, No. 3 (Summer 1972), 141–51, ably argues for the appropriateness of interpreting this lecture in the light of James's other writings. James's consistency on this issue may be viewed as partial confirmation of Dooley's suggestion, but we shall see more confirmation in what follows.

To avoid tedious repetition, I shall sometimes refer to our "passional nature" as our "passional" *side* or simply as the "passional," without any change of meaning.

3. James is aware, therefore, that he is referring, not to some "intrinsic property" that makes any particular hypothesis "live," but to the relationship of any such hypothesis to the "mind" of an "individual thinker," a relationship that makes it plausible to that thinker's mind. For the relevance of these remarks, see the treatment of John Hick's objection in chap. 4, below.

4. *E contra*, James goes on to suggest somewhat disconcertingly that an hypothesis which a "chemist finds live enough to spend a year in its verification" would rank as a "trivial" hypothesis of the sort that "abound in the scientific life [WB 4]"! Rather than taken as a put-down of science, this should shock the reader into seeing what James means by an hypothesis that is truly "momentous."

5. Observe that later on, having re-established the rights of the volitional to enter into the believing process, James alludes in passing to the possibility that Pascal's Wager argument may be a "regular" clincher," after all [WB 11]. Merely a rhetorical flourish, that admission? Or a sign that James's attitude toward the Wager argument, and possibly toward Pascal more generally, was an ambivalent one? See my discussion of this question below, chap. 3.

6. Analyze the tightly woven summary of his argument presented on WB 7, and it is possible that James means the adjective "vile" to characterize Pascal's Wager argument; but the characterization holds only if Pascal is interpreted (or caricatured) as James, *at this precise stage* in the development of his own case, and *for the purposes* of developing that case, makes free to interpret him. Did James mean this interpretation to stand as his last word on the Wager and on Pascal? See above, note 5, and below, chap. 3.

7. James groups Arthur Hugh Clough and Thomas Huxley with, but aims his fire mainly at, W. K. Clifford, who had written in his "The Ethics of Belief" the series of propositions James quotes from him. This was a chapter in his *Lectures and Essays*, edd. Leslie Stephen and Frederick Pollock, 2 vols. (London: Macmillan, 1879); see pp. 182–86. I elide (as not directly relevant to this stage of the argument) what James more precisely means by the "opposite extreme" these men prided themselves on embracing: the pessimistic view that the "incorruptibly truthful intellect ought positively to prefer" that the cosmos be a dark and disconsolate place, as though the "bitterness and unacceptableness to the heart" implied by that view must somehow be taken as positive guarantee of its truth. He

quotes (perhaps maliciously) Clough's jingle that: " 'It fortifies my heart to know / That, though I perish, Truth is so—' " (WB 7). More recently, of course, the fashion calls for Albert Camus' comparably pathetic "We have to imagine Sisyphus—happy."

8. James here alludes (WB 9) to a number of "volitional" factors —belief, fear, hope, pressure, partisanship, etc.—that go to make up the intellectual climate of any time and place, but he makes no attempt to be more than illustrative when doing so. Nor does he confront the need for discriminating among their obviously uneven claims to "legitimacy"; he is, after all, merely setting up the question he means to deal with focally. But one could have hoped that, in another lecture perhaps, he might have dealt more attentively with the nest of problems raised by his enumeration; see below, chap. 7.

9. Nor, James points out, are the hypotheses involved in such scientific "options" truly "living" ones *for us* as "spectators" of the scientific game, though they *may* be living options for the passionately commited scientific researcher. There is an anticipation here of Thomas S. Kuhn's later distinction between the creative and the more "routine" kind of scientist; see WB 20–21 and Kuhn's *The Structure of Scientific Revolutions* (Chicago: The University of Chicago Press, 1962; rev. ed., 1970), esp. pp. 52–65.

10. The meaning of "forced" seems to have gone through a shift in James's mind: it is no longer merely a question of the disjunction's leaving no (logical) "middle ground"; now the (more existential) consideration has entered whereby the choice must be made *now*, without postponement. That exclusion of postponement was, however, formerly a feature of the option viewed as "momentous," so that James has not surreptitiously imported a consideration not included in his original premisses.

11. The quotation is actually from Thomas Huxley, but taken as associated with Clifford's contention in the same sense; see above, note 7.

12. Despite his sympathetic views on the possibilities for "human immortality," James does not make those views operative as premisses in WB. The point has bearing on whether he is encouraging us to engage in "wishful thinking"; see below, chap. 4.

13. Compare WB 30–31, SR 96, and LWL 59. The metaphor seems clearly to have resonated with his personal experience of, and predilection for, the challenges of mountaineering. See TC I and II passim, esp. I 377–78. Again, Dooley's prescription (see note 2, above) proves a sound one.

2

On Matter and Manner

IT TAKES a certain shamelessness to present the kind of content analysis of James I have given above, however necessary it may be. I have tried to highlight those features of his lecture which have become the focus of subsequent discussion about its cogency, or lack of it. But in doing so, what a sense of embarrassment, almost of desecration. For all the hearty flavor, the genial electricity, of James's contagious style is drained away in the process.

Not everyone would deplore such a reduction of this full-blooded address to the dry bones of its matter and argumentative sequence, but a Jamesian "believer" must. For central to all James's philosophical activity is the conviction, which features so prominently in this lecture, that the *whole* person must be engaged in philosophic exploration, not merely the pure intellect or logicizing reason. *Cor ad cor loquitur*, Newman never tired of reminding us: if "real" rather than merely "notional" assents are his concern, the thinker must be willing to present himself in all the fullness of his humanity, feeling and sensitivity included—and, one must add, human vulnerability as well. In that self-presentation, style is no mere ornament; style is the man.

But it must be admitted that James's style has worked both for and against him, and never more tellingly than in "The Will to Believe." Nowhere more vividly do we catch that mobile, darting, adventurous quality of his mind, his artist's responsiveness to the folds and curves, the rock-ribbed massiveness, the darks and glints, of reality which elude the everyday eye. Not only do his early experiment with the painter's vocation,[1] and his wide and responsive

reading in literature and poetry of every stripe,[2] represent
a backlog of "mental equipment," a stock of lively illustrations, but both interests are profoundly symptomatic of
the kind of thinker he was fated to become. Even in his
more technical *Principles of Psychology*, we know we have
met the man himself; but in his popular lectures, this "Hi-
bernian"[3] propensity, this sheer reveling in "good talk,"
sprightly and humorous, serious and solemn by turns, is
fully unleashed. Even at those junctures when we simply
must cry halt, and slow his ebullient progress with a question, an objection, a demand for more precision, a smaller
voice within us murmurs its "almost thou persuadest
me. . . ."

But there are such junctures; precision, logic, cogency
are not solely matter for impatience or scorn. And it must
be admitted that the nether side of James's style asserts
itself exactly here: his early mockery of the "laboratory"
psychologists disclosed his own lifelong impatience with
the plodding unromantic toil of getting it precisely right;
and the way he virtually blazoned a superficial conver-
sance with logic and mathematics betrayed that streak in
him which, Perry tells us, was "profoundly opposed to the
whole life of scholarship," amounting even to a "temperamental repugnance to the processes of exact thought."[4]

This congenital weakness in James's otherwise impressive philosophical armory may serve as some excuse for
the arid summary I have presented of "The Will to Believe"; but it should not excuse anyone from direct
acquaintance with the lecture itself. While tracing its argumentative line as faithfully as I could, I have also
attempted to point, even if allusively at times, to the slips
and gaps that have fueled the discussion of later scholars,
both critics and advocates of James. Before moving on to
that scholarly discussion, though, one major caveat is
called for. James can be headlong and charming, impatient
with technicities; and his thought comes attired in a style

of matching cut. But it would be fatal to conclude that he was not "serious" about the issues he was airing, here and in the other popular lectures of this period of his career. Debonair always, he was continents removed from being cavalier.[5]

The point has its importance, and the weight one feels entitled to assign to this phase of James's activity depends upon getting it clear. For one eminent critic has come dangerously close to questioning that seriousness. John Hick prefaces his treatment of "The Will to Believe"[6] with a "pilot study" of Pascal's "Wager"; that very association, which James himself may be thought to have invited, along with Hick's own evaluation of Pascal,[7] may have influenced his judgment. But in any case, Hick's analysis leads him to the conclusion that James entertained an "essentially sporting" attitude toward religious belief.[8] James does, it is true, revert to the language of the gaming table toward the end of his lecture—and that despite his earlier dismissal of such thinking as unworthy and perhaps even "vile"; Hick is also correct in pointing to James's allusive appeal to similar expressions in "The Sentiment of Rationality."[9] But place those expressions once more into their larger context, take account of the adversaries James is dealing with, then grant him the right to his personal lecturing style, and surely a more generous interpretation than Hick's suggests itself. Life itself involves risk, and the human person's total commitment in religious faith is surely one of life's largest risks: the betting metaphor, even if Pascal's classic argument had never given it general circulation, would come naturally to mind to express that risk. But a metaphor it remains, and James's remarks on Pascal's use of it show his lucid awareness of its limping inadequacy. Speak in sporting metaphors of life, and of religious faith, and only the most literal-minded would infer that you take the game of life as just another game.

But there are risks and risks, and James's adversaries

would have it that the risk of falling into error is so "solemn and awful" a thing that no thinking being should be willing to court it. Now the word risk has taken a somber turn; the gaming-table sort of risk has become only its pale image. It is James's task to show not only that the risk of faith commends itself, but that his adversaries, instead of offering us a life without risk, would have us risk all the meaning of our human lives through a timorous submission to a one-sided epistemological rule, a rule that would dissuade us from "doing the [personal] universe the deepest service" we may be called upon to offer. We are worlds away from the gaming table now, and if "sport" is involved, it is deadly serious sport.

But that last phrase quoted from James's "Will to Believe" suggests an aspect of the faith-commitment which Hick, like so many others, has totally ignored. He has been perspicacious enough to see that an interpretation of this lecture may set off a hunt through its companion lectures from this period of James's production; but "The Sentiment of Rationality" is only one of a number. What light do the others shed on James's attitude toward faith?

Hunting down an answer to that question will occupy us further on. To set the stage for a fuller answer to Hick's objection, as well as to light up other facets of "The Will to Believe," a word on this phase of James's philosophical effort is in order.

"[R]eligion," James remarks in a letter of 1897, "is the great interest of my life . . ." (*Letters* II 58). That interest went back to a significant degree to the influence of his father, Henry James, Sr., whose energetic career as writer, lecturer, and marathon conversationalist was fiercely dedicated to religious questions.[10] James's touching devotion to his father went along with an unfeigned admiration for the man, even if it never brought him into complete agreement with his views. But that paternal influence was as incalculable as it was inescapable; soon after his father's death, summing up what would "stay by [him]" of all his father bequeathed, James included "the sense of his right to have a say about the deepest reasons of the universe" (*Letters* I 221). Specialize though he did in physiology, then psychology, as early as 1865—when 23 years of age—James pledged himself " 'to study philosophy all [his] days,' " and remarked, eight years later, that his " 'interest [would], as ever, lie with the most general problems' " (see *Letters* I 53, 171). Perry writes of him that "From his adolescence James was both fascinated and tormented by ultimate problems. . . . he was haunted by a cosmic nostalgia—by those deeper doubts and hopes which are the perpetual spring of religion. He felt these emotions both in his own behalf and vicariously in behalf of every sincerely troubled human soul."[11] As late as 1907, James expresses his delight that his friend Carl Stumpf is " 'working more and more into metaphysics, which is the only study worthy of Man!' "[12]

It was, in fact, this exalted notion of philosophy that almost kept him from being a philosopher at all: his " 'strongest moral and intellectual craving,' " he writes to his brother Henry, " 'is for some stable reality to lean upon,' " whereas the professional philosopher's *business* seems to pledge him " 'publicly never to have done with doubt on these subjects, but every day to be ready to criticize afresh and call in question the grounds of his faith of the day before. . . .' "[13] This once seemed too lacerating a calling for one who for so many of his younger years had "brooded upon the nature of the universe and the destiny of man," and for whom these questions were "vital" questions.[14] That gnawing preoccupation with the deepest and most cosmic of questions, Perry suggests, may have contributed in part to the neurasthenic depression, and near-collapse, that brought James so low between his twenty-sixth and twenty-eighth years.[15] It is significant that James himself attributed his "rebirth," in large part, to the

bracing assurance he gleaned from reading Renouvier's
Deuxième Essai: man's will is perhaps genuinely free, after
all, and not the inconsequential plaything of a universe
whose physical laws determine its every act.[16]

Many of the seeds of James's popular lecture on "The
Dilemma of Determinism" are already detectable in this
earlier experience;[17] but, one may ask, why was precisely
this conviction so vitally important to him? The reason lies
in one of the differences James always had with his father's
views: his father, he was persuaded, too easily resorted
to a higher, aesthetic resolution of the problem of evil, a
resolution that, in James's view, sapped at its very root the
efficacy, importance, and deepest seriousness of human
moral activity.[18] In later years, this would be his objection
to, and the driving motive of his unrelenting assault on, all
forms of "Hegelism" as he understood it.[19] His early adoption of the "empiricist" attitude went along with the hope
that scientific "fact" could be reconciled with the validity
of religion.[20] Life, he was convinced—and paradoxically,
his reading of his father's friend Carlyle made strongly for
that conviction—is a "real fight," against real evils, and
humankind's resolute will to engage in the fight makes a
real difference to the ultimate outcome.[21]

The pages of James's popular lectures are sprinkled
with references to and quotations from Thomas Carlyle,
all breathing the same spirit of fighting ardor he had im-
bibed from Carlyle's writings. "What was the most important thing he said to us?" James asks the audience of his
"Dilemma of Determinism": "He said: 'Hang your sensibilities! Stop your snivelling complaints, and your equally
snivelling raptures! Leave off your general emotional tom-
foolery, and get to WORK like men [DD 174]!'" This is the
no-nonsense language of the "strenuous," or "serious,"
moral mood (MP 210–13; cf. LWL 47–51, 54–59) James
always held forth as the only mood worthy of a human being, a mood he so often expresses in martial metaphors and

calls to battle. This same man, toward the end of his career, deliberately set about an extended study of the military experience, in preparation for his eventual essay calling upon mankind to wage the battle for peace as a "moral equivalent of war."[22] "The Energies of Men," says Perry rightly, is nothing less than an essay on "the psychology of heroism," a topic that always fascinated James. "What Makes a Life Significant?" asks the title of another such lecture, and the answer comes: "courage, struggle, risk— in a word, heroism. . . ."[23] One of his most telling thrusts against the Cliffords and the Huxleys was that the materialistic universe their science might bequeath us could offer no ultimate support for the heroic dedication to truth to which they summoned us![24]

For heroism must be fueled by the "vital heat" of a fighting faith:[25] James's personal religious belief always wore this moral, even moralistic, battle-dress; this, and his accompanying conviction that we may not lay the existence of evils, any more than their final conquest, at the doorstep of an "infinite" God, partially account for the arm's-length he always kept between himself and every form of institutionalized religion.[26] God himself could be enhanced by man's uncompromising fidelity to the call which such a "melioristic" universe laid upon him; it did make sense to speak of a "deepest service" one could pay to that universe.

This, I suggest, is the fuller, rounder resonance that such terms as "risk" take on when James employs them; alongside the stern and martial risks of this cosmic battle, the risks of the gaming table give off a tinny echo, and sports of any description shrink to puny metaphors.

When, by the time he was thirty-five, James had become a popular figure on the lecture platform, he acceded eagerly to the invitations that came his way. The income which would help him further his children's education had something to do with that. But more significant is what he made of that opportunity. It offered him quite literally a platform to have his say, at last, "about the deepest reasons of the universe," to share his own "cosmic nostalgia," and deal with the deepest, most general problems that, his own experience convinced him, were of vital importance to others as well. He returns, in a word, to the topic that had always been the "great interest" of his life: religion.

He had always admired in his father not so much the "philosopher" of religion as the "prophet"; he now takes up the succession, donning his own prophetic mantle with accustomed grace, and delivering his message in a vernacular spiced with the same verve and dash as always flavored his conversations. But his seriousness is evidenced by the cluster of topics he chose to deal with: in 1877, "The Sentiment of Rationality";[27] in 1879, "Rationality, Activity and Faith";[28] in 1880, "Great Men and Their Environment"; in 1881, "Reflex Action and Theism"; in 1884, "The Dilemma of Determinism"; in 1891, "The Moral Philosopher and the Moral Life"; in 1895, "Is Life Worth Living?" and in 1896, "The Will to Believe." By 1899, James has been invited to give the prestigious Gifford Lectures. Health problems force a delay; but he has already decided upon the topic he intends to treat, and is snatching every well moment to get ready: *The Varieties of Religious Experience* is the fruit of that stubborn labor.

All the lectures mentioned above contribute, each in its way, to our understanding of "The Will to Believe." For they all serve to illumine a range of questions which, on examination, turn out to be one closely related family of questions, if not, at bottom, the same fundamental question orchestrated in a variety of registers. They all concern themselves with the most general "cosmic" terms on which human life, as James sees it, "makes sense"; they all reconnoiter the impact the "religious dimension" has on that vital human question; they all propose, as crucial to settling that question, the appeal of a moral life lived in the serious or "strenuous" as against the genial, "easy-going" mood; and cumulatively they support the conclusion that it is reasonable to believe in the religious dimension which, James is convinced, is indispensable for sustaining that moral mood.

" 'Religion,' " James writes in 1873, " 'in its most abstract expression may be defined as the affirmation that all is *not* vanity.' "[29] That "all," for him, embraces the most precious values humankind has come to cherish; for if religion itself is vanity and humans have no right to believe in it, then our sentiment of rationality is a liar, the universe makes no sense, we are not genuinely free, morality is an illusion and heroism the posturing of witless idiots, and the sort of life this leaves us with is certainly not worth living. We must not let his manner deceive us; the man took these matters with ultimate seriousness. If the whole man was mobilized in his address to these questions, the whole man was equally engaged in grappling with them.

NOTES

1. Ralph Barton Perry, *The Thought and Character of William James*, 2 vols. (Boston: Little, Brown, 1935), I 201, 459 (hereafter cited as TC).

2. TC I 260–73.

3. Perry's genial characterization, TC I 128.

4. TC I 442; II 680.

5. James himself acknowledges, in a letter to Shadworth Hodgson dated December 18, 1881, a paralogism uncovered in his RA lecture; see TC I 620. One is free to think his reaction in this instance was less troubled than it might have been, but generalizing from that instance would fly in the face of the array of evidence Perry adduces for the seriousness of James's attitude toward the topics of his popular lectures. On the term "popular," see *Works* xii–xiii; it does not mean "casual."

6. In *Faith and Knowledge*, 2nd ed. (Ithaca, N.Y.: Cornell University Press, 1966), pp. 33–35; the critique of James's lecture runs to p. 44.

7. See below, chap. 3.

8. *Faith and Knowledge*, pp. 40, 42.

9. Ibid., p. 40. This, however, is the only other popular lecture Hick brings into his study; that limitation seriously affects his estimate of James, as we shall see.

10. Perry devotes extended attention to this early relationship with Henry James, Sr.; see TC I 3–165.

11. TC I 450.

12. Given in TC II 203.

13. Quoted in TC I 343.

14. TC I 323.

15. TC I 322ff. Quite probably there were other, less conscious factors that accounted for this depression, and James himself may have been too ready to overintellectualize the matter. See, for example, the suggestive (but, at points, highly conjectural) article by Marian C. Madden and Edward H. Madden, "The Psychosomatic Illnesses of William James," *Thought*, 54, No. 215 (December 1979), 376–92.

16. TC I 323; see also James's letter to Renouvier given in TC I 661–62.

17. Including the axiom that the first act of a free person ought to be that of affirming that freedom (DD 146).

18. TC I 143.

19. TC I 727.

20. TC I 449–62, 501.

21. TC I 143, 159.

22. TC II 271–78.

23. TC II 270.

24. TC I 503, II 210; cf. PP II 640.

25. TC II 324; cf. 353.

26. TC I 471.

27. Though not published until 1879, "Most of this [essay] was written in 1877" (*Letters* I 203).

28. This lecture was later incorporated into SR (see TC I 495 and SR 63).

29. Quoted in TC I 503, II 448.

3

James and Pascal

THE QUESTION of James's seriousness in proposing his thesis on the "will" to believe might eventually have surfaced on its own, but the fact is that John Hick's astringent criticism of this lecture brought it dramatically to the fore. Crucial to Hick's case are his view of Pascal's Wager argument and what he presumes was James's attitude toward that argument.

Hick begins his study of James's lecture by instituting a brief "pilot study" of Pascal's Wager. This way of proceeding, however much encouraged by James himself, already supposes a kinship between the Wager and James's "will" to believe; in any case, it may have served to highlight, for Hick, features in James's argument which naturally send the mind back to its family resemblances with the Wager. It is striking, for example, how tirelessly Hick worries the objection that James had an "essentially sporting" attitude toward the ultimate issues of belief (p. 40);[1] that he regards faith as a "prudent gambler" would, whereas the ordinary religious believer brings to faith an attitude "entirely different from that of the gambler" (p. 42). References abound to "risk" and "risking," "winning" and "losing," "staking" and "backing," and it is symptomatic of Hick's perspective that his only reference (p. 40) to another of James's popular lectures is to the passage in "The Sentiment of Rationality" where James speaks of the "total game of life" in which we are obliged to "stake our persons all the while."

This preferential stress, I suggest, may initially have arisen from James's introductory allusions to Pascal's

Wager; but it may also have been exacerbated by Hick's own estimate of that passage in the *Pensées*. He assures us that the Wager assumes a view of our cognitive capacities such that the problem of God's existence must be dealt with in the same way as we would deal with the question whether "a coin will fall head or tail at a particular throw." Pascal, therefore, has likened the option to believe or not believe to a "game of chance"; we all live in a "cosmic gambling den" and are forced to wager one way or the other, and Pascal advises us to make the wager which may gain us everything but which, if we have bet on the wrong side, will lose us virtually nothing (p. 34).

Conceive of God, Hick goes on, after the model of some "touchy Eastern potentate," invisible, but publicly advertised as "inordinately jealous for homage," and Pascal's argument might well be a "rational form of insurance." It costs us nothing to make a reverence to his apparently empty throne, even if he does not exist; whereas if he does exist, we may have "saved our lives" by thus placating him! These "barbarous earthy terms" into which the Wager "translates so readily," Hick sums up, betray its "essentially non-religious character." The conception of the deity which it implies has "shocked many readers" since Pascal first published it (p. 34).

Thus far Hick's formal presentation of Pascal's Wager. Granted: his introductory remarks warn us that Pascal himself seems to have proposed the Wager, not as a "normal path to belief in God," but rather as a "final and desperate attempt" to move the "almost invincibly apathetic unbeliever." It does not, then, represent Pascal's own "central thinking" about belief in God, and, Hick speculates, the *Pensées* in the finished form they never came to assume would have seen Pascal hedge his Wager with all manner of "safeguards and qualifications" (pp. 33–34). One wonders, though, whether Hick himself has kept these caveats in mind, for he soon goes on to characterize the Wager in the bald and repellent terms quoted above.

More to my point here, however, is the fact that Hick seems not to have credited James with any great awareness that such caveats might be in order. He solemnly intones that the Wager's "implied conception of the deity" is rightfully shocking, and adds, without a break, that "William James has used the same basic idea" of God, as though it were "consonant with Christian theism" (pp. 34–35). Then, with spectacles so tinted, Hick turns to a discussion of James's lecture.

With that set of lenses, it is not altogether surprising that Hick caught in his sights the "sporting," "gambler" James he was predisposed to see. There is, of course, more to Hick's criticism of James than I have summarized here; the other points he makes will occupy our attention further on. My purpose now is to focus on that precise aspect of his critique which springs from the kinship, as he sees it, between James's argument and Pascal's Wager. The point I hope to make is this: a more careful study of the *Pensées*, combined with a wider and more sensitive appreciation of James's attitude toward that work, warrants our drawing conclusions quite the reverse of those which Hick would urge upon us.

It is worth noting, to begin with, that James seems to have enjoyed a lifelong familiarity with the *Pensées*, a familiarity that strikes the reader as warmly sympathetic, on the whole. That kind of familiarity one would expect of anyone educated in a French culture; its absence would surprise almost as much as an American's ignorance of Tom Sawyer or of the Gettysburg Address.[2] It comes, then, as less than startling that James, who received so much of his early education abroad, and notably in Geneva, can allude to Pascal, even quote him, as easily and naturally as he does. *Malgré les misères qui nous tiennent par la gorge*: he cites the phrase in the most unforced fashion, especially when ruminating on the "greatness and misery of man." For that was the Pascalian context in which it occurred in Charles Louandre's edition of the *Pensées*,[3] a copy of which, annotated—so the editors of his *Works* assure us (254n16.6, 259n29.7)—with a series of marginal comments and cross-references, was found in his personal library. The above quotation occurs in a letter of 1869, during James's famous period of depression, and was penned only shortly before he set himself to reading Charles Renouvier's *Deuxième Essai*. That historical context is significant, as we shall see very shortly.[4]

James had, therefore, a more than ordinary familiarity with Pascal's *Pensées* and a lively interest in that work. And yet, we may guess that he felt a certain resistance to Pascal as well. For James's entire religious orientation was anti-orthodox and anti-institutional, while Pascal was pleading for the inflexible orthodoxy of that superbly institutionalized religion, Roman Catholicism. James's religious set was staunchly Protestant, and here was Pascal, defending the religion of "masses and holy water." Such stuff might do for his Irish maid and Italian grocer, but a Harvard type of the 1890s could recognize benightedness when he saw it; James fully expects that same acknowledgment from those satellite luminaries at Yale and Brown. Why, one would as easily succumb to the seductions of the Mahdi. . . .

And yet, Pascal has gotten into his blood; he cannot overcome his fascination for the man. His thoughts volleyed forth like flaming arrows, scarlet with passion yet crystalline with intelligence; his style, so unequivocally "the man," admirable, endearing, pathetic, was so much what the Jamesian style would become; and here was a mathematician of genius depreciating, or at least severely calling into question, the primacy of a form of thought which James found so alien to his own personal bent. For the "reasons" that move the human being in matters of great moment are, Pascal declared, not reasons of head or brain so much as reasons of the "heart." This was one of the most cherished and frequently proclaimed insights of that prophetic character Henry James, Sr.;[5] it was a conviction that deeply marked his son—so deeply that one is tempted to view his philosophical career as one sustained endeavor to codify what his father had intuitively seen.

James's ambivalence toward Pascal translates into a profound ambivalence toward his Wager argument. In his first treatment of it, in fact, he is quite as searingly critical as Hick is. The context of that early treatment is important, however: James is preparing his auditors' minds to question their own conviction that our volitional natures should never be permitted to influence our acceptance of any truths, whatever their nature. The precise point he concedes to them, momentarily, is the contradictory of what he will eventually prove; after summarizing the Wager, he concludes that all such Pascalian talk of "believing by our volition seems, then, . . . simply silly" (WB 7).

His description of the Wager is, in part at least, a deliberate caricature, calculated to encourage that false conclusion. Pascal is trying to "force" us into believing by reducing our concern with truth to a gambler's interest in a "game of chance"; for "A game is going on between you and the nature of things which at the day of judgment will bring out either heads or tails" (WB 5). He has anticipated Hick's metaphors, and they cut with the same critical edge. His audience must feel, James goes on to observe, that this gambling metaphor implies that the apologist for belief has been put to his "last trumps"; a faith adopted on the basis of so mechanical a calculation would "lack the inner soul of faith's reality." His final observation is devastating: if we were God, we should rightly take a mordant delight "in cutting off believers of this pattern from their infinite reward" (WB 6). Can this be the man who, Hick assures us, "used the same basic idea," the same "touchy Eastern potentate" conception of God as Pascal's Wager? Indeed, is Hick's criticism of the Wager, when all is said, any more acid than James's was before him?

But it must be conceded, perhaps in Hick's favor (but only perhaps), that James now slues off and aims his critique at Pascal's religion of "masses and holy water"; this, he assumes his auditors will agree, is no longer a "live" option for enlightened Protestants like themselves, any more than the Mahdi's appeal for their trust and worship would be. Hick makes some reasonably solid points against this phase of James's argument, which I shall deal with further on. But what may have faintly encouraged Hick in setting up his hasty equation between James and Pascal is the series of more sympathetic remarks James later comes to make on the Wager argument.

Having conceded to his audience as much as he thought was their due—that allowing our volitional nature to influence our acceptance of truth would be, in the number of instances at least, either "silly" or even "vile"—James goes on to argue that there are other instances in which our volitional nature does, in point of fact, wield such an influence. There are, therefore, "passional tendencies and volitions which *run before* . . . belief" (WB 11; emphasis added), he concludes. In the light of that conclusion he now reverses his field and admits that "Pascal's argument, instead of being powerless, then seems a regular clincher. . . . The state of things," therefore, "is evidently far from simple . . ." (WB 11).

At this precise point in his lecture, James gives formal expression to the thesis he means to defend in the remainder of his talk. One of the central points of that thesis comes down to affirming that "Our passional nature not only lawfully may, but must," in certain instances at least, "decide" matters for us (WB 11; emphasis deleted). Not only does our passional nature *de facto* intervene in the formation of certain beliefs, but there are instances in which it *must* so intervene, and therefore *lawfully, de jure,* may so intervene. Perhaps, after all, there was some validity in Pascal's way of arguing!

This brings us to the other, more sympathetic side of James's ambivalent attitude toward the Wager, and to Pascal more generally. And here, again, he anticipates Hick to a remarkable degree. The Wager, James knew well, was by no means all that Pascal had written even in his *Pensées.* Pascal's own personal belief, he avows—even if it be in masses and holy water!—must have had different roots; hence, the Wager must have been an argument aimed at others, a "last desperate snatch at a weapon" forged against hardhearted unbelievers.

It comes as no surprise, therefore, when at a pivotal juncture in his lecture, James appeals (WB 21) to that celebrated Pascalian adage "The heart has its reasons, of which reason knows nothing." For to compare the *worth* of things, he goes on to say, "we must consult not science, but what Pascal calls our heart. Science herself," in fact, "consults her heart" when judging that factual knowledge is worth our having, indeed, is one of the "supreme goods" humans can strive for (WB 22).

"The heart has its reasons": that phrase has often been used to justify wishy-washy sentiment, mindless love-conquers-allism, anarchic feeling as arbiter on any and every question. Indeed, there are instances where one suspects that some such understanding commands James's own interpretation of the phrase.[6] But James knew better; I hope it will come clear further on in this essay that he did so. To make that clear, however, one is well-advised to begin with what Pascal himself meant by the "heart" and by its "reasons."

This is the very tack, it would seem, that James himself took: his personal copy of the *Pensées* shows that he wrote in page references to three additional occurrences of the term *coeur* (*Works* 259n27.9);[7] one may surmise that he saw the term as important for Pascal, that it caught his interest, and that he may well have been trying to find some common thread of meaning running through these various uses of it.

It would be idle to pretend that Pascal had any single *technical* meaning for the term: he was not that kind of writer. But it is still possible to locate a "field" of meanings, and with enough accuracy to exclude what he did not mean and to divine what a reader like James might find him suggesting.

Pascal's spiritual kinship with St. Augustine is a matter of record. One would fully expect, then, to uncover analogies between his *coeur* and Augustine's *cor*; thus, it is not surprising that for both of them the "heart" is the seat from which the "inner man" beholds and responds to the higher world whence God addresses his call to fallen human creatures. But to hearken to that call fallen creatures must recognize both their "grandeur" and their "misery," the wretchedness into which they have been plunged, and (in the phrase we have already seen James use), despite the "miseries" which "clutch us by the throat," the "irrepressible instinct which raises us upward."[8] That recognition carries a feeling-charge, but it is a recognition; it has genuine noetic character and value. "Reason" functions, not in opposition to, but alongside, the heart, or, more exactly, subordinated to it; reason functions at its best, in fact, when directed by and responsive to the urgings of the heart. Reason is unable, for example, to prove the "first principles" which guide it in its operations: the heart alone can intuit and approve of them. So, in one of the passages James lists in his annotations, "it is on the knowledge supplied by the heart and instinct that reason depends, founding thereon all its utterances."[9] Or, in another phrase that caught James's attention, "We know the truth not only through reason, but also by the heart."[10] How, then, to translate the phrase from this same context *"C'est le coeur qui sent Dieu, et non la raison"*?[11] The usual translation runs, it is the heart that "feels" God, not reason, and surely Pascal is intimating the feeling-charge that accompanies that apprehension, when the heart is properly *sensible*, "sensitized" to God's call. But *sentir* is just as much a noetic term; it expresses an apprehension, but the kind of loving apprehension of which reason is incapable. This is the meaning to be given to the famous phrase "the heart has its reasons, of which reason knows nothing." Those "reasons of the heart" are the farthest thing from blind and mindless sentiment.

So Pascal can pen that lapidary *pensée* that says merely "heart, instinct, principles."[12] The heart's intuition of "principles" is an "instinctive" grasp, as "natural"[13] as the heart's "love" for both itself and the Universal Being. The Pyrrhonian skeptic, whom Pascal brings repeatedly into his sights, is capable of questioning even that fundamental intuition; he can argue that our lives may be merely a dream, that space, time, motion may not be real.[14] But this merely reminds us that humans can fight against their basic God-given "instincts"; for "nature" is fallen, and the "heart" itself can be corrupted.

Heart, nature, instinct: Pascal adds another member to this family of terms. He speaks of the will directing (and legitimately directing) the operations of the mind, somewhat as "heart" is entitled to do. At this juncture we come very close to James's own "will" to believe. "The will," writes Pascal,

> is one of the principal agents of belief; not that it creates belief, but because things are true or false according to the side from which we look at them. The will, preferring one aspect to another, turns the mind away from contemplating the qualities of things which possess qualities it does not care to see; and so the mind, walking in step with the will, stops to look at the aspect it likes; it comes to a stand before the aspect it prefers, and so it forms judgment by what it sees therein.[15]

Compare that proposition with this one, from James's personal notebook: " 'Free will,' " he writes, means " 'the sustaining of a thought *because I choose to*, when I might have other thoughts' " (quoted in *Letters* I 147). That phrase James entered into his notebook in 1870; he had just come across it while reading Charles Renouvier's *Deuxième Essai*. That reading made him credit Renouvier with his "rebirth" from the fearful depression that had held him under for two long years! The sentiment is, however, remarkably Pascalian in import.

But the context from which James drew it is even more remarkably Pascalian. To quote Perry's elegant summary of the matter: Renouvier was an empiricist who recognized the empiricist's "narrow and momentary certainty in the immediate presence of particular facts," and went on to stress "the discrepancy between this dubiousness of knowledge and the assurance of belief." Only the will, he argued, can ensure the "consummation of belief" that reason itself cannot ensure. But how to justify this leap to belief, this "premature and hazardous self-commitment," with its "excess of assurance over evidence"? The only justification possible is a moral one: "where experience and logic are not decisive, and where there is at the same time a practical need of belief, *there* belief may and should be dictated by moral and religious considerations." Perry goes on to relate Renouvier's claim that "As a matter of fact . . . all of the great philosophical systems *are* expressions of the temperaments and inclinations of their authors, however much they may profess to submit only . . . irresistible proof"—a contention that James cited in his notes, and then went on to incorporate into his personal thinking.[16]

Pascal, Renouvier, James: even if we do not subscribe, to the letter, to all Perry's interpretations, the genealogical traces are strikingly suggestive. Did James refresh his acquaintance with Pascal while working on "The Will to Believe"? There is excellent reason for thinking so. But quite aside from that historical question, the ineffaceable family resemblance between Pascal and James runs deeper than any suggested by Hick's polemics.[17]

That kinship only makes James's ambiguity toward Pascal's Wager all the more intriguing. His summary (WB 5–6) of the central portion of Pascal's argument is careful and fair enough;[18] but, even given the argumentative context, to say that Pascal is striving to "force" us into Christianity by encouraging us to equate our concern for truth with a gambler's concern for the outcome of a coin-toss is as unjust to Pascal as Hick is to James. But James goes on to make Pascal's argument conclude in this fashion: "Go, then, and take holy water, and have masses said; belief will come and stupefy your scruples,—*Cela vous fera croire et vous abêtira*. Why should you not? At bottom, what have you to lose [WB 6]?" Now this, one must protest, is entirely too offhand. Nor is the unfairness of James's characterization sufficiently offset by his admission that Pascal had concocted his argument for others than himself, for hardhearted unbelievers. Hick, we saw, uses almost identical language, except that, in one of his few departures from James's estimate, he describes the unbeliever as "apathetic" rather than as hardhearted.

Hick is closer: for Pascal is addressing,[19] not hardhearted unbelievers, but the torpid, rather, the unreflective, who day by day plod onward toward their death, without ever a sidelong thought to how that death will affect them. They live "distracted by distraction from distraction" as it were, or, in Pascal's own words, "indifferent to the pursuit of the truth of a thing so vital, and touching them so closely"; "unreflecting, undisturbed, they live without a thought of the final end of life . . . as if they could annihilate eternity by turning their thoughts away from it."[20] Men like this "must have lost all feeling" when they do not even "take the trouble to inquire" about a question so vitally important to them.

Add a few centuries, and Pascal's estimate of his audience is not all that different from the one James levels on his own: " 'I wish,' " he writes to John Jay Chapman, " 'you knew a few of the intellects *at* whom that speech was delivered.' " His lecture is " 'only calculated for the sickly hotbed atmosphere of the philosophic–positivistically enlightened scientific classroom,' " for " 'the victims of spinal paralysis which these studies superinduce.' " Chapman had implied that the "faith" James had challenged them with was not robust enough, and James agrees; but for patients of the sort he had to deal with, only a dose of " 'homeopathic treatment' " would do them any good. It must have seemed to Chapman a " 'poor little razor-like "thin edge of the wedge" which your academic personages twiddle between their fingers,' " but even such a mild cathartic " 'really does good.' " [21]

One does not, James is contending, try to catapult such victims of "spinal paralysis" from the anemic state they are in, in one unbroken arc, into the fullness of "robust" faith. But this was exactly Pascal's own view; it was buttressed by his orthodox conviction that Christian faith was a gift from God. That theological consideration need not have troubled James, but Pascal was also calling upon a psychological realism that should have appealed to him.

His method would have appealed to Chapman, for it is far less gentle than James's own. Pascal feels that such "spinal paralysis" victims as he is dealing with must be shocked, awakened out of their "strange insensibility to things of gravest import"; he must make them *sentir*, both "see and feel," the "extravagance and stupidity" of their benumbed condition, literally "confound them by making them see what madmen they are." The language of a "wager" is one they will at least understand.

But once Pascal's audience has been more accurately identified, it becomes clear that the Wager was neither the "last" nor the "final" argumentative tactic that James and

Hick, respectively, maintain that it must have been. It was much more, as James thought of his own lecture, a *first* step—more energetic and determined than James dared take, but only a first step. Pascal implies this when he writes: "Before embarking on the proofs of Christianity, I think it necessary to point out the wrong-headedness of men who live indifferent to searching out the truth of a matter so vital. . . ."[22] All he hopes to accomplish, even by this shock therapy, is to wake them up, get them to see that the question is there and that it concerns them dreadfully, jolt them into a reflective mood. Facing them with the "proofs" of Christianity before ensuring that attitude would be woefully premature. This is a long chalk from hoping that his Wager will "force" them to believe in God, as James puts it, or provide an argumentative "path," in Hick's milder term, toward such belief. Pascal is theologically too orthodox for that, and psychologically too astute.

But he does end his "wager" gambit with the recommendation James quotes: take holy water, hear masses. What does he mean by this? Pascal's auditor has protested that he is still "not free, not released" from the desires that turn his life into a round of mindless pleasure-seeking; "I am so made than I cannot believe. What am I to do?" "At least," Pascal replies, "acknowledge your impotence toward believing. . . . Do your best to gain conviction, not by an increase of divine proofs, but by a decrease of human passions." Follow the route others have taken before you, he counsels: they did everything "as if they believed—took holy water, heard masses, and so forth. Even naturally, that will make you believe, will stupefy you. . . ."[23]

"Even naturally": Pascal is convinced that faith is essentially a supernatural affair, a gift from God. But the human being's "natural" dispositions have something to do with the receptivity which normally provides the soil for that gift. Yet humans are a strange amalgam: of soul

and that body which Descartes, and Pascal after him, regard as a "machine." Surely the dispositions of the "soul"
are alone relevant in preparing the ground for God's gift
of faith? A strict Cartesian might agree, but not Pascal.
The gestures, actions, postures of the "machine" can pave
the way for analogous gestures and postures of the soul.
Genuflect, and you may think that only the bodily machine
has assumed this attitude of humility and adoration. But
no, the soul is humbled too and, from that posture of abase-
ment, begins to sense that adoration may not, after all, be
so unnatural an attitude for it to take on. This is not adoration yet, any more than hearing masses or taking holy
water is tantamount to full enjoyment of Pascal's Catholic
faith; but for someone whose life has been a tumult of
passionate desires, it "stupefies" both soul and body, and
places him in the stillness where the "heart" may hearken to
the call of God that conveys the gift of faith. "To look for
help from this outward act is superstition; to refuse to
combine it with the inward is pride."[24] Not bad theology,
that; not bad psychology either. As for the latter, one could
have hoped that the man who wrote the ageless chapter
on "Habit" in his *Principles of Psychology* might have
done it greater justice.

One final analogy: neither Pascal in his lengthy section
on the Wager, nor James in his entire lecture, deals directly
with the "content" and "grounds" of the decision to believe.
Pascal intended to postpone his "proofs" for Christianity
to a later portion of his "apology"; James restricts himself
to a highly abstract definition of "religion," and never
directs his audience's attention to the *matters* they might
mull over in coming to a faith-decision. Does finite being
entail the existence of an Infinite? Do the evils of our
universe argue against the reality of a God? Does our
world evidence traces of teleological design? We know
that James himself dwelt long amid such questions, and
that he found himself generally disaffected toward the

"traditional" proofs for God's existence. Was he merely reluctant to air such "content" issues?

The answer to that, I submit, is a clear "no." For James shows no reluctance, in the other popular lectures of this period, to invite his hearers to probe into the features of our human world—freedom, morality, the hunger for happiness—that he came to think spoke most eloquently for God's existence. But he had been brought to realize how decisively the *attitude* we bring to such considerations inevitably influenced the conclusions we draw from them. A good lecturer sets out to make one main point, and James was a master of the art. So, from beginning to end, he resists the urge to expatiate on *what* we might believe, and severely confines himself to showing, as he hoped, that matters of religious faith are peculiar in this respect: they may, and even lawfully must, be approached with a "heart" attuned to its own kind of reasons, with a predisposing "will" to believe. A limited point, when all is said, but one which, if valid, is well worth making.

To conclude, then: John Hick would have us read "The Will to Believe" in the light of Pascal's Wager argument, but as he himself interprets that argument for us. Look more carefully at Pascal, and at the relationship between Pascal and James, and Hick's counsel becomes darkly suspect. He has failed to bring into play the profound ambivalence James manifests toward both the Wager and Pascal's *Pensées* more generally. James's summary of the Wager's substance is surprisingly parallel to Hick's, and his initial estimate of its value, even if we allow for its contextual intention, is so acidly critical as almost to be unfair. But he is bending over backward to show his auditors how well he can understand their prejudice against all such volitional views of belief; it is only when he has softened, and then corrosively attacked, that prejudice that he unveils the more sympathetic view of Pascal's fundamental contention he has been backing the whole while.

Was Pascal, then, trying to "force" us into belief? It would be chancy to take this as James's last word on the matter; but it is mildly ironic that he characterizes the Wager as a "last desperate snatch" when close study shows it was more in the nature of an opening gambit. For the Wager, like James's entire lecture, was designed to shake and even shock self-complacent apathetics into adopting the attitude of "will" or "heart" which both men saw is required as the predisposition for sanely reflecting on the question of belief. All this is clear from the *Pensées* even as they stand; there is no warrant for Hick's speculation that in their finished form we might have seen Pascal hedging his Wager with all manner of "safeguards and qualifications." Indeed, that suggestion may well come from Hick's having unreflectively accepted James's suggestion that the argument is, as Hick puts it, a "final and desperate attempt," and not a predisposing shock treatment to get serious reflection underway.

But there is even less warrant for claiming—in fact, it is seriously unjust to characterize James's lecture as supposing—the same sort of barbarous deity as Hick finds implied in his skewed interpretation of the Wager, for James would have us, in his deity's place, quite cheerfully cut off such gaming-table believers from their ultimate reward!

James, then, is quite as critical of Pascal's Wager, and of the deity it might (taken out of context) be thought to imply, as Hick would have us be. Further, in reducing Pascal's religion to one of "masses and holy water," he is positively unfair: it should have been clear to him, with a little more attention, that a religion which came down to such posturings of "man the machine" would have little or no appeal for Pascal himself. But that dismissive caricature is probably symptomatic of James's resistance to a broader image of Roman Catholicism; it should not blind us to the lifelong sympathy, the lively fascination he brought to the study of the *Pensées*. For there is good reason to conjecture that Pascal's "heart" eventually translated into James's "will" and "passional" natures, and that the powerful charge which James attributed to Renouvier's *Deuxième Essai* was the more easily detonated because of the subterranean influence Pascal's *Pensées* had long been wielding on the deeper reaches of his mind.

Despite his surface disagreements, and one hasty moment of unfairness, James does greater justice to the deeper implications of the *Pensées* than he may consciously have intended. In the words Perry uses to characterize James's estimate of John Stuart Mill, he "builded better than he knew."[25] For, in a real sense, a sense quite different from the one Hick would have us countenance, he succeeds in reproducing a Pascal in modern guise. Addressing a contemporary version of Pascal's own audience, he treats them to a dose of homeopathic medicine, shocks their apathetic hostility toward believing anything beyond what the evidence clearly warrants, and makes a similar appeal to the "heart" and "will" as commanding and directing the work of reason. One could point to phrases in Pascal which foreshadow James's insight into the special character of options that are "forced" and "momentous"; one might even speculate on whether his appreciation of Pascal's persuasive powers did not prompt him to reflect on why this religion of "masses and holy water" held such minimal plausibility for his mind—why, in the term he invented to cover such a case, it was not a "live" option for him. But dealing with such issues would bring us far afield. We have seen enough to substantiate the view that, *pace* Hick, the "sporting" language of risk and wager veiled, for both Pascal and James, the passionate conviction that the game of life man plays out with God is deadly serious.

But if the relationship of James, Renouvier, and Pascal traced here is even approximately accurate, it raises a sur-

prising question. Admit for a moment that the Wager argument was Pascal's technique for exploding an affective
bomb that would predispose his apathetic reader to reflect;
admit that the Pascalian "heart" directs and commands the
workings of reason; assume, further, that James intends
the same predisposing effect and that his notion of the
passional side of our nature runs parallel with Pascal's
notion of heart, and it becomes distinctly possible that the
influence of heart, will, or passional nature would not
follow upon, but actually precede and command, the operations of reason's reflections on the "evidence" for God's
existence. Could anything more irrational be imagined—
and could this be what James is seriously advocating?

NOTES

1. Page references to Hick's *Faith and Knowledge* (cited in chap.
2, note 6) will, henceforth, be given in parentheses in both the text
and the notes.

2. The French and French-speaking Swiss had some firm notions,
in James's time at least, about required curriculum; some acquaintance with Pascal's classic would have been expected of every *lycéen*,
a presumption that James's easy familiarity with the *Pensées* serves
to confirm.

3. (Paris: Charpentier, 1861), p. 137. References to the *Pensées*
here are given to the now definitive edition by Louis Lafuma (Paris:
Garnier–Flammarion, 1973), which I abbreviate to L, with Lafuma's paragraph numbers; in this case, see L 227. James's memory
has elided the phrase somewhat. The original reads: "Malgré la vue
de toutes nos misères, qui nous touchent, qui nous tiennent à la
gorge . . ." and occurs on p. 137 of the Louandre edition, pp. 117
to 135 having treated of the "greatness and misery of man."

4. TC I 472.

5. TC I 149.

6. The series of sorites James later elaborates to defend the "will"
to believe (TC II 242–43) would at first suggest this interpretation,
and it remains a possible way of reading those particular soritic arguments. I find, however, the repeated presence of the term "ought" in
those sorites suggesting a deontological middle term that is essential

to the understanding of James's more authentic thought on these matters; see below, chaps. 7 and 8.

7. The references are to pp. 225, 374, and 237 of the Louandre edition. For more on these, see below.

8. L 227, already mentioned above, at note 3.

9. L 214 and Louandre, pp. 224–25; see note 7, above.

10. L 214 and Louandre, p. 224; see note 7, above.

11. L 225 and Louandre, p. 224; see note 7, above.

12. L 331.

13. L 224; cf. L 246.

14. L 214; for the context, see note 9, above.

15. L 375 and Louandre, p. 154.

16. TC I 656–58 esp. 657n13.

17. James's summary of the Wager, including the quotation, exactly rendered (WB 6), suggests he reviewed it while composing this lecture. Note also that to Renouvier, an empiricist-voluntarist-fideist like James, Pascal must have been philosophical mother's milk; he would have been ideally chosen to reinforce, or bring to the surface, whatever latent Pascalian tendencies James might have hoarded from his earlier education.

18. The Wager occurs at L 343, and Louandre, pp. 230–32.

19. See the note to this effect, written by Pascal's advocates from Port-Royal, at *Pensée* 434 in the edition by Léon Brunschvicg (Paris: Hachette, 1897); cf. L 246.

20. L 12; see also L 11.

21. Given in TC II 235–37.

22. L 12 (see also L 11). This, then, was Pascal's strategy, the "program" he laid down for himself in the *Pensées*. It is also unmistakably reflected in the first chapter of Louandre's edition (pp. 105–17), which immediately precedes and colors the reading of this passage.

23. See the illuminating note Brunschvicg includes (at the *Pensée* he numbers 233) to explain this *cela vous abêtira*; Pascal is playing richly on the term. The adoption of these pious external practices will both "tame" and "stupefy" Pascal's skeptics, reduce their pretensions that they are only being "reasonable" to the "stupidity" they really amount to, thereby making them the "children" they must become before any conversion is possible. For the true nature of their condition is that they are already both stupefied and stupid!

24. L 722 and Louandre, p. 239. Observe, in this connection, that the p. 237 to which James refers in his personal annotations (see note

7, above) is the finale of Pascal's argument on the body–soul inter-action in the growth of belief, an argument that runs over to p. 238. James's reading of p. 239, accordingly, was more than likely con-ditioned by this context.

25. TC I 561.

4

Is It "Wishful Thinking"?

THE RELATIONSHIP he thought he saw between Pascal's Wager and James's "will" to believe furnishes John Hick with the perspective he brings to his summary of James's entire lecture. In a surprisingly brisk two pages, he states its central point this way: there are risks on both sides of any genuine option; the believer risks accepting falsehood, but the skeptic who refuses or indefinitely postpones belief risks losing out on the truth and whatever practical good may accompany believing. So, James is saying, we are entitled to view our "stake" in the matter as important enough to grant us the right to choose which of these two risks we shall run. And James, for his part, chooses to risk that his "passional need of taking the world religiously might be prophetic and right" (WB 27).

So, Hick summarizes, James is asserting "our right to believe at our own risk whatever we feel an inner need to believe." "The Sentiment of Rationality" confirms Hick's view, and he quotes: "In the total game of life we stake our persons all the while; and if in its theoretic part our persons will help us to a conclusion, surely we should also stake them there . . ." (SR 94). Life is a gambling proposition, and faith is a sporting wager: this, Hick assures us, is the "essence" of James's argument (pp. 39–40).

Hick goes on to admit that James's appeal to the workings of interpersonal relationships is both "sound and important," but relevant only to faith in the sense of "trust," not to faith as a form of "cognition." Now his summary of James's case takes more sweeping form: if James's argument were essentially valid, then it would "authorize . . . us to believe ('by faith') any proposition, not demonstrably false, which it might be advantageous to us . . . to have accepted" (p. 42).

"Any proposition" that is "not demonstrably false": a number of Jamesian defenders, as we shall see, take issue with Hick at this point. For James insists that the option before the believer must be live, forced, and momentous; were we to attend only to those three properties, the class of propositions to which James's thesis applies would be far more limited than Hick recognizes. But, Hick insists, that set of restrictions does not truly extricate James from the argumentative hole he has dug for himself. Consider, as a test of this, the manner in which James dismisses Pascal's religion of "masses and holy water": to him, as to his nineteenth-century Protestant hearers, this does not represent a live option—he even goes on to equate it with belief in the Mahdi! But, writes Hick, all sorts of "accidental" circumstances may account for any option's being live for us and dead for someone else, by dictating the convictions, beliefs, or just plain prejudices that are "widely held in the society around us." An option that could, and possibly should, be live can simply have the life pummeled out of it. Thus, were we raised in another culture, the Mahdi's invitation could come at us with a more electric appeal than Protestantism, or Christianity more generally. Hence, any number of options that may be dead in one time and place may be live in another time and place; the restriction, Hick concludes, is "unwarranted." For the fact that a particular belief represents a live option to this or that person "has no bearing on its truth or falsity" unless we are willing to surrender to the absurdity that "truth varies geographically with the liveliness of local options" (p. 43).

The restriction is "unwarranted": we shall have to see whether this is the best expression for what Hick has in mind. For the moment, though, let us continue to follow his argument, for now it takes a revealing turn. A "purely rational mind," he goes on to say, "liberated from the accidents of geography and illuminated by James's [own] argument" would have to find it just as rational to accept the Mahdi's invitation to faith as the Christian invitation which James just happens to find more live to his New England Protestant mind. By the logic of his own argument, Hick cannot see how James could "consistently refuse" the Mahdi's invitation. Why? Because, says Hick, "the mere thought of what might be gained if a proposition is true will automatically render it a live option to us," whatever part of the world we live in. All that is required is some "self-assertive person"—like the Mahdi—"who offers a heaven and threatens a hell" to make any option "live" for us; indeed, "the more stupendous the promises and threats, the more justified the belief" (pp. 43–44). Whatever James's own intentions may have been, accordingly, the "logic of his argument" constitutes no more than an "impressive recommendation of 'wishful thinking,' " authorizing the conclusion that "we should all believe in that religion or philosophy which we most desire to be true," "we may believe what we like," and "while we are about it we had better believe what we like most" (p. 44).

Whatever one may think of its value, Hick's criticism has succeeded in provoking reams of impassioned discussion. For the moment, though, it should be noted that he arrives at his remarkably economical distillation of James's argument, first, by ignoring a number of refinements that James considered important to making his case, and, secondly, by lifting his proof-quotations out of the refining contexts that lend them their exact point and bearing on the argument.

To convince us, for example, that the "essence" of James's argument comes down to the quasi-Pascalian wager of risk *vs.* risk, Hick quotes (pp. 39–40) a paragraph in which, it must be admitted, the language of risk, stakes, and "getting on the winning side" (WB 26–27) features prominently. But the force of what James is arguing in that paragraph cannot be appreciated unless one recognizes that he is now applying two points which he has previously made and which he considers vital to the conduct of his argument: (*a*) that the "scientific skeptic" may not be portrayed as the defender of intellectual sobriety as against the believer's preference for passional irresponsibility—for the skeptic has made an equally passional choice: only it is one that erects as its primary epistemological rule "avoid error" as against the believer's more positive rule "gain truth"—and (*b*) that, accordingly, the passional side of our nature *may* be "prophetic and right" —noetically sounder—in its preference for taking the world religiously.

A similar distortion of meaning occurs in the reading Hick gives of the section from "The Sentiment of Rationality": for there James is arguing that the *whole person*, not just the "theoretic part" of our natures, is involved in the kind of choice being made for belief or non-belief. So, if we trust those "inborn faculties" that belong to our passional side, and those faculties are "good," then we turn out to have been prophets, and our choice about a genuine option will then be "prophetic and right."

But all Hick can see in these two paragraphs is, not the central point James is making in them, but the offending language of risks and gaming tables. In boiling James's lecture down to this "essence," Hick has boiled too much of it away. Instead of asking why James himself thought this or that argumentative turn important, Hick has taken the tack, always dangerous when dealing with a first-class thinker, of assuming that a host of details are mere window dressing that can safely be ignored. This will become plainer when my discussion focuses on the "friendship" metaphor and on the double service to which James puts it; but for now, a good illustration of such singleminded obloquy is what happens to James's live option once Hick gets finished with it.

For when leading up to the climax of his refutation by *reductio ad absurdum*, Hick gives himself away: he has scored his triumph by working a gradual shift of meaning on the key term "live" option. What makes an option "live" for him? Hick answers: the "mere thought" of "what might be gained" or lost on one side or the other, the "heaven" that is promised or the "hell" that is threatened; so, the "more stupendous the promises and threats," the more "live" the option becomes. For in Hick's mind (and, he hopes, in the minds of his readers) an option is live in the exact measure in which the goods it promises make an "appeal" to our "likes" and "desires." But virtually any proposition, like the Mahdi's, can be fraught with such intense appeal: hence—to rephrase Hick's earlier conclusion—it is "unwarranted" to consider "liveness" as a requirement that would limit and reduce the number of genuine options that may exist.

To reach this astonishing conclusion, though, Hick has distorted the meaning James repeatedly assigns to the "liveness" of any proposition. It is, James tells us, one which "appeals" to him to whom it is proposed, but in what sense? His opening definition is unmistakably clear: it appeals as a "real possibility"; it must be "among the mind's possibilities" (WB 2). Hence, he can conclude by asking his auditors to reflect on whatever resistance they might still experience to his thesis that "we have the right to believe at our own risk any hypothesis that is live enough to tempt our will." For his auditors may be "thinking (perhaps without realizing it) of some particular religious hypothesis which for [them] is dead . . . of some patent superstition." But "living options never seem absurdities to him who has them to consider" (WB 29). The appeal to the "will" to which James is referring is limited, therefore, to options which, *prior* to having that kind of appeal, are real possibilities for the *mind*. Not any old promise will do, however stupendous, for it may require our believing a proposition which strikes our minds as "absurd" or a "patent superstition"; hypotheses like these, James asserts, are already dead for us, and "our willing nature is unable to bring [them] to life again" (WB 8). The proposition, to be live, must on the face of it appeal on the merits of its plausibility, in terms of the real possibility (which our thinking minds can recognize) that it may be *true*. Only then can that other range of appeals, to likes, desires, or dreads and fears, come into play. We are, then, *pace* Hick, "warranted" in viewing "liveness" as a characteristic that limits the number of genuine options that may exist. Wishful thinking may stretch very far; but James was lucid enough to see that its limits stopped well short of Hick's "demonstrably false."

And yet, Hick was on to something. He could have argued his point less maladroitly, but there remains a substantial point to his objection. For James admits that the liveness of any hypothesis is, not a property that is exclusively intrinsic to the proposition itself, but one that always involves a relation to concrete persons, living in a particular time and place. Moreover, he insists, those persons are not pure minds, abstractly theorizing intellects, but full human beings with a passional side to their natures: the whole "person," he contends, goes into the acceptance of any hypothesis as live, and into the rejection of competing propositions as dead. Furthermore, he points out that what makes certain options dead for us is "for the most part"—perhaps not universally, but in the majority of cases at least—"a previous action of our willing nature of an antagonistic kind" (WB 8–9). Those previous actions are not limited to "deliberate volitions," but include the less reflective acceptance of a welter of other influences which he groups under the label "intellectual climate." To this point, James has been detailing the factual state of affairs that obtains for all concrete human thinkers.

But what factors create any such intellectual climate?

James contents himself with listing some examples: "fear and hope, prejudice and passion, imitation and partisanship, the circumpressure of our caste and set" (WB 9). Undoubtedly there are others, but even limiting ourselves to those cited, we cannot help thinking that when compared one with another, they are crazily uneven in value. More than that, any one of them can take a multitude of forms: fears may be great or petty, fantastic or real, and so on. James does not seem to notice the Pandora's box he has so casually pried open, but surely a reflective hearer is prompted to move from this depiction of the *de facto* situation to the obvious *de jure* question: How legitimate is the varied influence these various factors wield on the formation of our beliefs? When is an appeal to our fears a valid appeal? To what fears? What kind of appeal? One could go on to probe passion, partisanship, caste, and all the rest: James has half-attentively thrown out a question that calls for conscientious discrimination, and merely left it to lie there wriggling before our gaze.

But discrimination is called for from another quarter as well: What are the factors that go to make up our passional nature? James alludes in passing to "wish and will and sentimental preference" (WB 8), but tells us very little more than that. But here again, even that incomplete enumeration raises similar issues of uneven value, unequal claims on legitimacy. May not my "will," for instance, sometimes rightly direct my mind to "sustain a thought" that runs counter to my "sentimental preference"? James's own formula for human freedom is on the line, and he scarcely seems to notice.

But could James have come up with a satisfying answer to these objections? Could he, for instance, reply to Hick that, once we discriminate the factors making up both our passional natures and societal climate of opinion, we can evolve norms for judging certain options as not only *de facto* but *de jure* live or dead? My suggestion in the following chapters will be this: that James not only could, but actually did, go a long way toward answering these and a number of other objections that have been proposed to "The Will to Believe"; and that most, though not all, of those answers can be drawn from a careful reading of his other popular lectures from this same period. Those may seem large claims; how can one even begin to redeem them?

A good first step might be to confront the objection which Hick has raised in its most formidable terms: that James's lecture provides us with a shameless license for "wishful thinking." For Hick, as he surely knew, was far from the first to raise this objection; it has a long history. In one of its forms, it was first proposed by a good friend of James's, and an otherwise sympathetic colleague, Dickinson S. Miller, writing very soon after the publication of James's lecture.[1] Miller took his stand on grounds very close to those of W. K. Clifford, the main target of James's attack in "The Will to Believe": it is our "duty" as rational, intellectual beings to evince a greater "sobriety" toward evidence than James was recommending. For if James were to be followed faithfully, the will to believe could turn into a " 'will to deceive—to deceive one's self; and the deception, which begins at home, may be expected in due course to pass on to others.' "[2] The philosopher, when it comes to such questions as God's existence, must consider not only his personal advantage or disadvantage, but the " 'good or harm . . . for all those concerned' "; for if he plays fast and loose with " 'the conscience of the mind, . . . the duty of being as intelligent as we can,' "[3] he can ignite a brush fire of like irrationality throughout society, and imperil the whole march of " 'human progress' "[4] whose advance presupposes just such intellectual honesty as he has called into question. No matter how live an hypothesis may be for us, accordingly, we must suspend our assent to it whenever the evidence fails to justify such assent.

It is not a mere irrelevancy to observe in passing that Miller was personally convinced that there was, in fact, " 'decisive evidence' "[5] with respect to the theistic hypothesis; and that C. J. Ducasse, who engaged him years later in an extended correspondence on James's contentions, was himself persuaded that the "gratuitous evils" of our world argued for his own atheistic position.[6] This, however, did not dissuade Ducasse from defending James's main contention, but as it might apply to cases other than the theistic hypothesis. He set himself to dreaming up a case to which James's thesis would apply, and he proposes it to Miller;[7] let him suppose himself

> "on a street car going down a hill when suddenly the brakes fail. There are then two possible things for a passenger to do: to jump off, or to stay on. But he does not know which of the two is more likely to save him from injury, and he cannot put off deciding which to do until he has consulted the records of other accidents. In such a case decision is and has to be nonrational in the sense of being instinctive, impulsive, temperamental, instead of based on in your words 'a rational gauging of the exigency.' "[8]

Now, the option involved here is clearly "genuine," Ducasse implies: the opposite alternatives are certainly "live," and the decision to be made a "momentous" one. And the option is "forced." Here Ducasse profits from the fact that the term "forced," even during the course of James's lecture, slides from its original "logical" meaning (involving two and only two mutually exclusive propositions) to the much more existential meaning arising from a situation " 'in which we cannot suspend decision between Yes and No . . . because to refuse to decide is then automatically to be deciding.' "[9] We cannot, therefore, follow Miller's counsel to suspend assent. The streetcar example proves that " 'there are cases of this sort in which evidence' " for deciding one way rather than the other " 'is either totally lacking to us or is equally balanced,' " and yet decision is forced upon us.[10] Ducasse is correct in what he says about this slide of meaning: the need for deciding now, and not delaying, James originally made part of the "momentous" option; but he later spoke of it as though it *were* entailed by the theistic option as, on the *practical* level, "forced."[11] Another imprecision in his lecture, if you will, but one toward which both Ducasse and Miller are ready to be indulgent, and rightly so.[12] The real point for investigation, they implicitly agree, is whether the streetcar constitutes a paradigm in which James's contentions prove out as valid, after all.[13] Ducasse argues that it does: for " 'In such a case the decision is and has to be non-rational in the sense of being instinctive, impulsive, temperamental' "—it cannot, given the conditions laid down, be based upon the " 'rational gauging of exigency' " Miller had demanded. But, adds Ducasse, " 'non-rational' " must not too swiftly be equated with the " 'irrational' " whose brush-fire propagation Miller so legitimately deplored. Miller might also take comfort from Ducasse's additional conviction that a concession made about a case like this one " 'affords no basis whatever for choice one way rather than the other; for claiming, for instance, as I think James was temperamentally disposed to do, that the instinct of affirmation is sounder, wiser, more likely to pick on the truth, than the instinct of negation.' "[14] Choices like these, Ducasse is saying, are like the streetcar choice in being " 'pure gamble[s].' " If we trust the "instinct of affirmation," we shall opt for the theistic hypothesis: pure gamble on our part. If we trust the instinct of negation, we shall deny God's existence: gamble, equally pure. But gamble we must, so gamble we may: such " 'wishful decision[s],' " even in religious matters, are " 'not merely legitimate but unavoidable.' "[15] But Ducasse seems to be implying more: the side of the gamble James chose to bet on depended on his " 'temperament' "; temperament is decisive. When explaining the streetcar decision, he had broadened the alternatives: that " 'non-rational' " decision could be " 'instinctive, impulsive, temperamental,' " but no matter; whatever determined the decision one way or the other was a totally " 'non-rational' " factor. Ducasse has implicity told us how he, at least, would unpack that slippery Jamesian term, the "passional" side of our nature.

Though he never seems to have convinced Dickinson Miller, Ducasse himself was persuaded that he had elaborated a defense of "wishful thinking"—or wishful decision; the difference in terms is of little consequence. Though he would not agree with the proposition himself, he acknowledges the right of someone else to decide for the theistic hypothesis, once such a person has concluded that there is no preponderance of evidence either for or against it, that the decision is " 'unavoidable,' " and that the promised comforts of religion are there to be enjoyed. A ticket to a " 'fool's paradise' "? Perhaps; but one may legitimately judge a fool's paradise preferable to a " 'fool's hell.' " . . .[16]

Some years later, Stephen T. Davis provided some fresh insights on this "wishful thinking" question. Davis was discontented with the fact that James gives no examples of "genuine options" that are "specific" and "real" enough for us to test them; "he only cites broad, general themes, e.g. what he calls 'moral questions' or 'the religious hypothesis.' "[17] So, by a slightly different route from Ducasse's, he arrives at the same need to concoct a case amenable to analysis. By one of those freak coincidences one comes across in the history of thought, Davis hits upon a case that is an exact modern parallel to the "streetcar" case Ducasse had proposed: now it has to do with the very same predicament as it might affect a truck driver: his vehicle has gone out of control, and he must decide whether to jump or not. Davis later discovers that he had, quite independently, reduplicated Ducasse, and draws the conclusion that there may be, after all, only very few cases that fit the requirements of the "genuine" option as James had laid them down.[18] Perhaps Miller's fears of a brush-fire "spread" of irrationality were ungrounded, after all![19] Perhaps, too, Hick had focused so closely on what James had written about the option's being live that he failed to see how the other features of a genuine option imposed such tight limits on the one making the option as to obviate the danger of unbridled "wishful thinking" to which Hick had pointed.[20] Instead of entitling us to believe "whatever we feel the inner need to believe," James first enjoins on us the duty of ascertaining whether the proposition in question belongs to that very restricted number to which all the Jamesian criteria apply.[21]

But instead of there being only three, Davis points out, there are, in fact, four criteria required before we have a "genuine" option in the Jamesian sense. Alongside "live," "forced," and "momentous," now write the term "ambiguous," for in James's description of such an option he states that "it cannot by its nature be decided on intellectual grounds" (WB 11; emphasis deleted). Take explicit account of this "ambiguity" criterion, Davis argues, and the number of cases fitting all four requirements is even more dramatically reduced.

But how ambiguous must such an option be in order to justify a Jamesian decision on passional grounds? Davis refers to Bertrand Russell's epistemological principle in order to pursue that question: " 'Give to any hypothesis that is worth your while to consider just that degree of credence which the evidence warrants.' "[22] This brings him to outline the five different "evidence situations" Russell's principle suggests, and to settle on the one that seems to fit the "ambiguity" criterion. Suppose that "There is *no* evidence available relative to the truth or falsity" of any proposition "p"; it follows that there is an equal absence of evidence for and against "non-p." Or suppose that the evidence for proposition "p" is neither stronger nor weaker than the evidence for "non-p." Russell's principle would enjoin, in such cases, the "refusal to commit oneself at all":[23] he would proscribe any "right"[24] to believe at all—would have us, in other words, suspend assent much as Miller would.

But, Davis argues, James's argument is aimed directly at the *universal applicability* of such principles as Russell's: when the option is not only ambiguous, but live, forced, and momentous as well, the thrust of James's position is that such epistemological principles as Russell has enunciated may legitimately be contravened! One may not, to overturn James's position, merely repeat Russell's principle!

Does the streetcar case argue, though, as Ducasse thought it does, that the situation was so *totally* ambiguous as to be decidable *only* on passional grounds? Davis is not ready to make that claim: scientists, for example, could after study probably determine which option—jumping or staying aboard—would likely be safer, even if not entirely safe; it could be argued that the passenger should make as quick a calculation of his reasoned chances as he can, instead of entrusting himself to the pure gamble involved in a blindly passional decision. That argument would, of course, be based on an assumption: that such a reasoned calculation, no matter how hurried, would assure *fewer* chances of deciding wrongly than the purely passional gamble would. But since we cannot be sure of that assumption, the passional method of deciding would seem, even on purely epistemological grounds, legitimate and defensible.[25]

Now, there are a number of common assumptions running through this entire discussion of "wishful thinking." The first of them is that one can reach some clarity on the issue by reference to "The Will to Believe," and to that lecture alone.[26] But we have seen at a number of junctures the vanity of all such attempts; we must be ready to range not only through James's other popular lectures, but elsewhere in his works as well, in order to understand what he is getting at.

That wider acquaintance with James, however, calls into question several other assumptions shared by most of the participants in this particular debate. The first of them touches on that central term "wishful." Everyone seems to have assumed that all James had in view was the desirability of religion's being true, the "advantages" and "comforts" its truth—or more precisely our *belief* in its truth—would provide. How the term "wishful" would apply to the pessimist's decision to "trust" his "instinct of negation" rather than its opposite—a possibility raised by Ducasse, but never explored—is not immediately evident, to say the least. There is also that arresting remark James makes about "doing the universe the deepest service we can"; surely this suggests another side to the religious option that does not lend itself so easily to the more self-interested language of "wish," "comfort," and personal "advantage." There is a track worth following here, but, again, following it entails spreading our net beyond the limits of this single lecture.

A second questionable assumption: the writers we have studied thus far give various interpretations of what James must mean by our "passional" or "volitional" nature, but each of them supposes his own ability to unpack that Protean term correctly. Will, wish, liking, instinct, impulse, temperament; irrational, non-rational—all these terms have been thrown about in the discussion without its having even once been suggested that their application might be highly problematic, after all. Would it be worthwhile to look further into James's corpus in order to find out what he might have intended by that term? Not merely worthwhile, it seems the only conscientious thing to do.

Less commonly shared, but still pervading most phases of this discussion, is a third assumption: that James's sybilline phrase about an "option that cannot by its nature be decided on intellectual grounds" implies this scenario: the intellect must first go through its (presumably) dispassionate examination of the evidence, come to the conclusion that the evidence is indecisive and the question before it truly "ambiguous"—and then, but only then, the passional side of our nature is entitled to tilt the scales. The only epistemologically conscientious scenario, of course; therefore, the one James *must* have had in mind. But the unsettling truth of the matter is that James had quite another scenario in mind, as a look into his other writings will show. And he was serious about it.

That same phrase prompts another question: What did James mean by an "option that cannot by its nature be decided on intellectual grounds"? When Ducasse and Davis feel compelled to excogitate a "case" which James himself never offered as an example, their implied assumption is that James himself would have accepted that case as one to which he intended his thesis to apply. Davis, to do him credit, shows some tremors of uneasiness in this respect: James obviously had more "reflective" cases in mind than the split-second streetcar decision; and the streetcar decision itself may not be so "naturally" ambiguous—to a scientist, say—as it might appear to the streetcar passenger. But it behooves the scholar to ask whether James himself has given us clearer indications of the kind of options he was concerned with, and to which he meant his contentions to apply. Only then can we make any judgment on the validity of those contentions.

Both critics and defenders of James have raised a final question: Is he truly arguing for a "will," or merely for a "right," to believe? Answering their own question, they have then gone on to object that his commendation of the kind of precursive faith that can "create" future facts not only has nothing to do with proving our "right" to believe, but really distracts from, and contributes only confusion to, his main argument. Obviously, there is a close connection between these two issues; but so inextricably do they interweave with the preceding question about the kinds of option James is mainly interested in, that all three must be dealt with simultaneously. To that task I shall turn first.

NOTES

1. See Peter H. Hare and Edward H. Madden, "William James, Dickinson Miller and C. J. Ducasse on the Ethics of Belief," *Transactions of the Charles S. Peirce Society*, 4, No. 3 (Fall 1969), 115–29. The same periodical has also published several other useful articles on the question, including those of Stephen T. Davis, "Wishful Thinking and 'The Will to Believe,' " 8, No. 4 (Fall 1974), 231–45; and Dooley's "Nature of Belief," cited above, chap. 1, note 2. Of lesser importance for my purpose here is James L. Muyskens' "James' Defense of a Believing Attitude in Religion," 10, No. 1 (Winter 1974), 44–54.

2. Dickinson Miller, " 'The Will to Believe' and the Duty to Doubt," *International Journal of Ethics*, 9 (1898–1899), 173, as quoted in Hare & Madden, "James, Miller, and Ducasse on the Ethics of Belief," 120.

3. Letter of Dickinson Miller to C. J. Ducasse, January 20, 1943, given in ibid., 119.

4. Letter of Miller to Ducasse, undated, given in ibid., 123–24.

5. Ibid.

6. Ibid., 124.

7. Letter dated January 18, 1943—when Miller was seventy-five years old!—given in ibid., 116–18.

8. Ibid., 117.

9. Ibid.

10. Ibid.

11. See above, chap. 1, note 9.

12. Notice that this shift in meaning comes naturally, so to speak, once James establishes the equivalence, in *practical* terms, of opting for either atheism or agnosticism.

13. The implication would seem to be that there is a "family" of such cases, even if a very limited one.

14. Letter to Miller, cited in note 7, above, 117.

15. Dickinson Miller, *A Philosophical Scrutiny of Religion* (New York: Ronald, 1953), p. 13, as cited in Hare & Madden, "James,

Miller, and Ducasse on the Ethics of Belief," 121; emphasis deleted. At least, Ducasse goes on to argue, we gain the consolation of doing *something* when we gamble rather than not!

16. Ibid.

17. "Wishful Thinking and 'The Will to Believe,' " 238–39.

18. Ibid., 245*n*15; see also note 13, above.

19. Ibid., 235; see also Hare & Madden, "James, Miller, and Ducasse on the Ethics of Belief," 120–21.

20. Davis, "Wishful Thinking and 'The Will to Believe,' " 235. Hick's shift in the use of "live" eludes Davis.

21. Hick does enter the qualification (p. 42) that the believed proposition must not be "demonstrably false"; but Davis would be correct both in asking whether this limitation is sufficient to do justice to James's case, and in charging that Hick's final verdict (p. 44) is a wild overstatement.

22. *A History of Western Philosophy* (New York: Simon & Schuster, 1945), p. 816, as cited in Davis, "Wishful Thinking and 'The Will to Believe,' " 231.

23. Davis, "Wishful Thinking and 'The Will to Believe,' " 231; emphasis deleted.

24. Davis refers here to the distinction between a "right" to believe and a "will" to believe, drawn by Kennedy in "Pragmatism, Pragmaticism, and the Will to Believe," cited above, chap. 1, note 1. We shall see more on this distinction further on.

25. Notice that Davis has set himself the precise question whether passional decisions of this special type can be defended on "epistemological" grounds; that way of putting the question to James's lecture embodies a set of assumptions which call for examination.

26. Hick does refer to one section of SR, but that is where he stops.

5

Outcomes and Over-beliefs

THE TASK of ferreting out the implications of "The Will to Believe" led me swiftly to comparing it with the other popular lectures James delivered during this same period of his life, and no less swiftly to detecting several points of consistency that initially justified such comparisons.[1] The questions James deals with in these lectures are all intimately connected with one another; they all center on what he saw as the "most general" questions confronting the human inquirer, the "vital" questions that eventually compelled him to follow at last in his father's footsteps, and to hazard his own personal say about "the deepest reasons of the universe." But one can be more precise than that: as Perry puts it, James saw the "urgency of philosophical problems" as arising from the "conflict between science and religion," a conflict whose solution must be sought, not in a "conquest" by one side over the other, but in a "reconciliation" of their competing claims.[2]

"The Will to Believe," just one step among many toward the reconciliation James was seeking, is aimed squarely at a central epistemological problem at issue in this same conflict. It should scarcely surprise, then, if its most authentic commentary must be drawn from the other steps he took along that same road.

The mere recall of the titles he gave those lectures, though, is enough to show the *kinds* of questions James was haunted by. They are all of the *weltanschaulich* order, probing whether our entire universe makes sense or not. This should already suggest that the kinds of options he is talking about in "The Will to Believe" might be of a similarly *weltanschaulich* sort. But we are fortunate in being spared the need to rely on such inferences, however obvious they might appear, for James has settled the issue for us. Writing to L. T. Hobhouse some eight years after the event (*Letters* II 207), in a coinage of his own he explains the kind of "beliefs" he had in mind: they were, he tells us, "over-beliefs," a term he leaves undefined, but expects his correspondent to understand without undue technical analysis. The same term appears in the notes James penned in preparation for the Gifford Lectures, given some two years before: the " 'mystical overbeliefs,' " he writes, " 'proceed from an ultra-rational region,' " from the " 'irrational instinctive part, which is more vital' " than " 'articulate reason.' "[3] The connection between over-beliefs and the passional nature of his earlier lecture on belief is transparent. But then, in a letter to H. M. Kallen, dated in 1907, James distinguishes between a first kind of belief " 'which produces verification' " by " 'produc[ing] activity creative of the fact believed,' " and a second kind which " 'may, without altering given facts, be a belief in an altered meaning or value for them.' "[4]

Now, the first kind of belief to which James refers here is plainly the kind he earlier illustrates by the plight of the Alpinist and the challenge of the train robbers. Both have their parallels in the streetcar and truck-driver cases concocted by Ducasse and Davis. Let me designate the common strand running through all these cases by terming them "outcome" illustrations. For in all of them we are asked to consider a belief as prompting the choice of one alternative over its opposite—jumping, for example, instead of staying—and in all of them we may judge the soundness of the guiding belief on the basis of its eventual outcome. One feature of James's theory, in other words, would have us base our judgment of the belief on whether or not it did in fact produce the kind of action "creative of the fact believed."

By the time he wrote that phrase to Kallen, however,

eleven years after delivering "The Will to Believe," James had come to distinguish that first kind from a second order of beliefs, which he now terms "over-beliefs": they do not "create" the facts of their own verification or even alter the facts in any way, and yet, they can cue the believer into seeing in the facts a "meaning or value" different from that which another observer might feel entitled to read out of them.

It takes no great leap of the imagination to guess that what James means by over-beliefs is identical with the kind of *weltanschaulich* views that earlier concerned him in his popular lectures. Adopt the view that man is free, that the universe makes moral sense, that life is worth living, or that God exists, or, as James would insist you should, adopt the entire interwoven nest of them, and you assume a viewpoint on reality which will inevitably "stage-light" the facts in such a way as to elicit a meaning and value from them which your fellow-humans might not decipher.

Some eleven years after delivering his lecture, therefore, James has become explicitly clear on the difference between these two orders of belief; it has also become clear to him that his original argument should have been aimed more unambiguously at justifying over-beliefs. Yet even when he gave that lecture, the distinction between beliefs and over-beliefs was not entirely unknown to him; his problem seems to have been that he had achieved only a blurred clarity about it, and about its implications for his argument. In opting for freedom over determinism, for example, he affirms roundly that "the facts practically have hardly anything to do with" our making that choice. "Sure enough, we make a flourish of quoting facts this way or that. . . . But who does not see the wretched insufficiency of this so-called objective testimony on both sides [DD 152]?" Indeed, when it comes to deciding issues like theism vs. atheism, idealism vs. materialism, monism vs. pluralism—all over-beliefs, surely—the facts surveyed by opposing parties "still face each other, and the facts of the world give countenance to both" positions (SR 107). What decides the issue for us, then, is precisely this: we all bring different "faiths," different "postulates of rationality" (DD 152), *to* our survey of the facts. The faiths we allow to color or weight the facts on either side make us all "peculiarly sensitive to evidence that bears in some one direction" (SR 92); we all "insist on being spoken to by the universe" (SR 89) in different, and highly personal ways.

By the time he gave his lecture on belief, then, James had come to an explicit conviction about the status and influence of what he would later term over-beliefs. His problem was that he did not possess a matching clarity about the distinction between such over-beliefs and the kind of belief that fuels our action in outcome cases. His later insight entitles us to interpret "The Will to Believe" as *de jure* directed toward justifying our adoption of certain over-beliefs; but taking that view of his lecture entails cutting through the *de facto* confusion he creates by repeatedly ignoring the difference in kind between such *weltanschaulich* options and the decisions we may be called upon to make in outcome cases.

Stay for the moment with just two of the outcome cases James proposes. His point in appealing to them is clear: the lively belief that the abyss can be vaulted, or that one man's opposition to the robber band may incite his companions to similar effective opposition, will certainly have much to do with the successful outcome of the action to be taken. But here James, faithful to his future-oriented empiricist stance, is contending that examples from practical life illustrate that faith can "create" the subsequent facts that can stand as its eventual verification. That claim, even as it bears on outcome cases, is not without its difficulties, as we shall see; but it is only fair to note that James's use of outcome cases is plainly different from the use to which Ducasse and Davis put them. It is one thing to say that in

streetcar predicaments I may be thrown back on the need
for resorting to a totally "non-rational" method of deciding; it is quite another to propose that if a lively faith
animates the decision to act in a certain way the outcome
is likelier to be in accord with what I desire. James may
have encouraged both Ducasse and Davis to think in outcome terms, but not in the *way* they came to think of them:
as though such cases represent the kinds of issue to which
James, at his alertest, intended his main thesis in "The Will
to Believe" to apply.

James's use of outcome cases, then, was illustrative of
the kind of faith that can "create" the facts of its own verification. Do they mean to illustrate how our faith can have
a similar "creative" role with respect to the theistic hypothesis? It is not at all clear that James always took the time
to analyze the issues involved here and to test whether the
parallel really held. Hick has taken that time (pp. 37–39),
and writers[5] more sympathetic to James correctly concur
that there is a confusion, if not a fatal flaw, in James's
thinking at this juncture.

Examine, for instance, the interconnected set of propositions embodied in his popular lectures: they come down
to affirming that the existence of God is the rock-bottom
assurance that life in the "strenuous," rather than the
"easy-going," moral mood is the kind of life which ultimately makes "moral" sense.[6] But the proposition that God
exists, *prima facie* at least, claims to tell us "what *is* the
case," now, in the existing arena of our significant human
activity.

The "experiential" quality of this argument for belief
in God's existence is, on one level at least, obvious enough:
James would have it that such belief will make a difference
in the tone of our activity and in the quality of our human
lives "even now." But there is a second level to be considered as well; one has to distinguish between "what *is* the
case" and what one "*believes* is the case." Immediately the

question arises: Has James set himself to proving that "it is the case" that God exists, or that we have a right, perhaps even that we would be better off, to "*believe* that God exists"? On a third level, hovering uncertainly somewhere between the foregoing two, is the question: If belief can sometimes create the facts that serve as its verification, does James mean to imply that our belief can make it "true" that God does, in fact, exist?

At this point, I submit that James's commitment to empiricism seems actually to have gotten in his way, introducing confusions into his argument which need not have beset him. In the first place, his empirical bent has led him to make an appeal to outcome examples, as illustrations of his argument, and momentarily to ignore the basic difference *in kind* between outcome and *weltanschaulich* questions. That faith can (and ought to) influence the outcome of human action is surely true, but if it has *any* influence on the truth or falsity of *weltanschaulich* propositions, it must surely be a vastly different kind of "influence." My belief that I can vault this chasm, and that my fellow-passengers will rise with me to foil the train robber, will surely make a difference in whether, and how successfully, I perform both those actions. Faith, in such instances, will have a bearing on the outcome, on what "will be the case." That James's somewhat bumptious optimism brings him seriously to entertain only the *successful* outcome is something to notice, surely, but I do not think it the main point for the present. The main point is this: he gives only the slightest attention to the linkage between what (one believes) "is *now* the case" and what "*will*, or *can*, become the case."

This loose linkage between present and future may have been what led one interpreter of James to argue the validity of his position, if only one substitutes "hope" for "belief."[7] But this defense of James really gives his case away: I can, certainly, hope that my wife will recover from can-

cer, without committing myself to the stronger claim that
I believe she will so recover. Such a hope, too, will have
a bearing on whether and how I move into action; its pragmatic value—for the style of *my* activity, if not for my
wife's eventual cure—is assured. But is it quite as efficacious as a hope which is founded on genuine belief? I
scarcely think so. There are hopes and hopes, and their intensity and consequent pragmatic efficacy will vary at least
to some extent with the varying "grounds" I have for hoping this or that. Those grounds bring us back to a consideration of the grounds for believing, and belief must
inescapably focus on what "is now the case." A firm belief
that my wife will recover must root partially at least in
some realistic appraisal of her present state. To believe that
I *can* vault some Alpine crevasse is to believe not only in
what "will" be, but to some extent in what "is *now* the case."
I may not have the muscular tone for it, the residual adren-
alin; in brief, the *present actualities* that underlie *present
potentialities* may simply not be *there*. And their absence
may be so complete that no amount of screwing up my
courage, "willing" to believe, will do the trick. Similar considerations apply to the train-robber example: I just *may*
have been stuck with a crowd of human cabbages, and no
amount of believing otherwise can wring the blood of
heroism from these blocks and stones. Granted: I may
believe that a successful outcome will ensue, my action
may be successful, and thus "verify," in James's terms, my
former belief; but the verification will bear on the truth
of my former belief in what, then, actually *was* the case.
This, I submit, is a much more modest claim than the one
James so often makes when assuring us that belief can
"create" its own verification.

In making that claim, too, James's professed empiricism
comes into play, but now it is compounded by the energetic, up-and-doing side of his nature. Notice how his
choice of these two examples—an Alpinist's leap, a bold

act of foiling a robbery—tends to stress the qualities of energy, courage, decisiveness: he wants us to grasp the nettle firmly, and so defy its sting. These are precisely the situations in which the very firmness of our "belief" is most often pragmatically effective. It was, I suggest, typical of James to survey the possible examples of belief and instinctively hit upon that subset in which energy, optimism, and courage enjoy greatest play.[8] And yet, it must not be totally forgotten that the very examples he stresses, the examples that serve the energetic side of his thesis best, do indeed call for that title word "will."

Even in outcome cases, therefore, faith may not always create its own verification. But James's failure to distinguish outcome options from their over-belief counterparts now introduces a second level of confusion. The most glaring instance of this occurs in "The Sentiment of Rationality," where James is addressing himself to the question whether our universe "makes sense," by which he means "moral" sense. He produces a number of distinctions and observations which I need not go into now; the point is that, on the face of it, he is entertaining a *weltanschaulich* much more than an outcome question. But he cannot overcome the temptation to treat the *weltanschaulich* question in outcome terms. He asks us to consider the whole mass of "mundane phenomena" ("M") as a conceivably indeterminate mass awaiting the further determination ("x") of our subjective attitude toward it. Our attitude may be optimistic or pessimistic; typically, this means we may "brave" rather than "give way to" the evils of the world; the outcome will be dependent on the action ensuing from our attitude "x." "This world *is* good, we must say, since it is what we make it,—and we shall make it good. . . . M has its character indeterminate. . . . All depends on the character of the personal contribution x." So, in a provisional conclusion, he declares: "Wherever the facts to be formulated contain such a [personal] contribution, we may logically, legitimately, and inexpugnably believe what we desire. The belief creates its verification" (SR 101–103).[9]

Here, I suggest, his eagerness to be empirical, coupled with his energetic optimism,[10] brings James to endow our activity with the magical power to make the universe what we wish it to be: i.e., to transform it from an indeterminate *M* to the kind of "*M* plus *x*" we desire it to be, and to believe that our personal contribution can make it so become. But suppose, the critical reader is prompted to object, the original *M*, however indeterminate we *believe* it to be, *is*, in actuality, determinate *enough* to resist our powers to transform it in this desired direction? We are faced once again with the possible gap between what *is* the case and what our powers may be able to effectuate as the *future* case, and in this provisional conclusion, James's enthusiasm permits him to leap that gap too airily. Can our belief, however energetically it invigorate our action, endow that action with the power to "make" the world make sense? Or "make" it be true that God exists?

James's terminal conclusion in this same essay shows him in a far soberer mood. It *may* be that the original *M* is not, after all, the "moral universe" my subjective attitude *x* supposed it to be; hence, if "I mistakenly assume that it is, the course of experience will throw ever new impediments in the way of my belief"—indeed, will foil, baffle, and eventually counter-verify it (SR 105–107). When it comes to issues of this breadth, therefore, the gap between what I *believe* to be the case and what *is* the case, and the associated gap between what *is* the case and what my believing action can effectuate as the *future* case, may be too sizable for spanning, after all.

Before arriving at this chastened conclusion, however, James makes another move to bring the *weltanschaulich* option into line with an outcome option. This time he is dealing with the issue of factual verification, so close to his empiricist heart. He sees that verification in the two sorts of cases will differ in one important respect: the position he is arguing against, he admits, is not of the kind that "can be refuted in five minutes"; questions of this type "defy ages." For in settling this sort of question "corroboration or repudiation by the nature of things may be deferred until the day of judgment" (SR 95). He admits having

> written as if the verification might occur in the life of a single philosopher,—which is manifestly untrue. . . . Rather should we expect, that, in a question of this scope, the experience of the entire human race must make the verification, and that all the evidence will not be "in" till the final integration of things . . . [SR 107].

Compare this verification situation with that of such outcome examples as the Alpinist or the truck driver, and another important difference surfaces. The question of whether to leap or not leap in both these cases can, in principle, be decided in "five minutes" or even less, as soon as the outcome one way or the other becomes clear, even if only to the protagonist in his last moments. The "belief" in question either creates its factual verification or it does not; the facts of the outcome are what one can quickly judge by. And our judgment after the fact implies, among other things, an estimate by hindsight of what actually *was* the case at the instant the truck driver or Alpinist made his decision.

James seems to be sensitive to this difference in the above quotation: the "hindsight" judgment proper to outcome issues is still being invoked, but now with the admission that it can be leveled only at the end of time. But then, of what use is this view of the outcome to any of James's own readers, asking themselves whether it is *now* the case that the world we live in makes moral sense? Put more strongly: isn't this judgment-day verification so indefinitely deferred as to amount to a dodge, a verification inaccessible by very definition, hence (for the empiricist, at least) no verification worth talking about?

If we accept James's later assurances that "The Will to Believe" should have been aimed more accurately at justifying such over-beliefs as those we bring to the theistic hypothesis, then we must admit that his way of appealing to such outcome cases as those of the Alpinist or the train robbers is seriously misguided: such scenarios serve to illustrate, from practical human affairs, his claim that an intense and energetic belief can "create" the facts that verify it and he assumes, altogether too readily, that the same or sufficiently similar "creative" property may obtain in regard to belief in the theistic hypothesis. In making this assumption, he tends to vault over two associated gaps: the first, between what I believe to be the case and what in actuality is the case, and the second, between what is now the case and what my action can, from out of what is now the case, "make" to be the future case. That logical leap is made somewhat easier for him by the very choice of outcome examples he chiefly attends to: they both put a premium on the voluntaristic qualities of energy, optimism, bravery, and decisive rather than reflective action, and encourage him in talking of the "will" to believe and precisely that. But his choice of examples aids his argument in another way: they camouflage his assumption that a *weltanschaulich* option may be "verified" in essentially the same ways as the outcome cases of the sort he has proposed as illustrations. Eventually, he must postpone that verification until judgment day, which is tantamount to abandoning the appeal to verification altogether.

But James's unexamined equation between outcome beliefs and over-beliefs of the more *weltanschaulich* kind wreaks severe damage in another quarter as well: it goes far to obscure a distinction that is vital to the legitimacy of his claims. For in arguing for the intervention of our passional nature, he tells us that such intervention is legitimate whenever the option facing us is genuine, but adds the proviso that the issue in question must be one that "by its nature" cannot be resolved on "intellectual grounds" (WB 11). This has brought a number of his defenders to infer that, in addition to their being live, forced, and momentous, James intended to qualify genuine options by including this fourth criterion, the criterion of "ambiguity." Their instinct is correct, but the application they go on to make of this criterion is, I submit, misdirected.

For that misdirection it must be said that James himself bears a large measure of responsibility, since it arises from his defenders' having been duped by his blurry equation of outcome with over-belief issues. Keep that distinction sharp, however, and it promptly becomes clear that the ambiguity proper to an outcome situation, like the Alpinist's or the truck driver's, is of a different order from the ambiguity affecting *weltanschaulich* questions. I shall call the outcome type, for want of a better term, an "accidental" ambiguity, meaning that it is not essentially unthinkable that either truck driver or Alpinist might be in total command of the facts relevant to making the decision to leap or not. That is why it is *in principle* possible to decide in terms of subsequent outcome facts whether they made the correct decision or not; indeed, as Davis himself has admitted, a scientific study might remove the ambiguity of the situation to a large extent. Any judgment made on such decisions, accordingly, can and should be made in terms of "the facts," and only command of an insufficient array of those facts infects their decision-situation with ambiguity.

But now, taking a cue from Perry[11] as well as from James himself, let me term the ambiguity proper to a *weltanschaulich* option a "necessary" or essential ambiguity. Let this be a provisional interpretation of that phrase in "The Will to Believe" which speaks of an "option [which] cannot by its nature be decided on intellectual grounds." In deciding such options, the "facts" themselves are not only ambiguous, but irremediably so. As we have seen James put it already, the "facts practically have hardly anything to do" (DD 152) with such options, for "the opposing theories"—whether determinism and indeterminism, theism and anti-theism, moral and non-moral universe —"still face each other, and the facts of the world give countenance to both" (SR 107). In the assumption that his later thinking would have persuaded James himself to set aside his appeal to a judgment-day "factual" verification as illegitimate, how would he propose that we resolve such *weltanschaulich* options?

Dear old James, one is tempted to sigh, how typical of him: that incorrigible averseness to the tedium of careful analysis has turned his brave lecture into a sad shambles. Is there any point in going on with this? There is, I suggest, great point in going on. We have managed to shear away some missteps, but when compared with the real contribution James has made, they may turn out to be of secondary importance. An appeal to "belief," the reader asks, quite in the Jamesian manner? To some extent; but the decision to terminate relations now might turn out to be Jamesian as well, but too like James in his impatient mood.

But the man himself kept thinking about these matters; his later ruminations, no doubt nourished by the controversy stirred up by his lecture of 1896, brought him to see that his argument should have been aimed more cleanly at justifying over-beliefs, the positions we assume on *weltanschaulich* issues. Such issues confront us with an ambiguity, surely, but an essential kind of ambiguity, of a different order from the accidental ambiguities that hover about outcome options. We may take it, then, at least as a working hypothesis, that he still saw the intervention of our passional nature as valid in the case of genuine options characterized by this sort of essential ambiguity.[12]

But when examined closely, even the few texts we have seen arguing for that essential ambiguity raise another, and troubling, question: At what point in our intellectual examination of the "facts" is the passional nature entitled to intervene?

NOTES

1. See chap. 2, pp. 30–31, and chap. 1, notes 2 and 13, respectively.

2. TC I 501; see also 494–503.

3. Quoted in TC II 328.

4. Given in TC II 249.

5. See, for instance, Robert J. Roth, s.j., "The Religious Philosophy of William James," *Thought*, 41, No. 161 (Summer 1966), 249–81, esp. 255–56.

6. This "moral" note is struck most clearly in RA and MP, but once alerted to its centrality in James's thinking, the reader can find it pervading all these popular lectures.

7. See Muyskens, "James' Defense of a Believing Attitude in Religion," cited in chap. 4, note 1.

8. I have omitted from this discussion any reference to the two illustrations James offers (WB 22, 28) about the formation of friendships. My reason is that they require more shaded treatment than the ones we have been dealing with, as we shall have occasion to see further on in this study.

9. Compare this passage, which dates from 1877, with LWL 59–62, dating from 1895, where James proposes essentially the same argument.

10. Many of the points made here have already been made by John E. Smith in *The Spirit of American Philosophy* (New York: Oxford University Press, 1963), pp. 38–79; see esp. pp. 56 and 76.

11. Who in TC II 209 points out (as Jamesian) the analogous distinction between "accidental" and "necessary" agnosticisms.

12. The text from James's preparatory notes for *The Varieties of Religious Experience* (cited in note 3) commends the realism of this hypothesis by linking " 'mystical overbeliefs' " with the " 'ultra-rational,' " the " 'instinctive part' " of our nature.

6

The Precursive Force
of Over-beliefs

GAIL KENNEDY, in an article to which I have already made allusion, argues that James's original lecture succeeds, in part at least, in defending a "right" to believe—a realization that James himself would appear to have come to some years after he had delivered it.[1] Given the essential sort of ambiguity affecting over-belief issues, this suggestion might seem to provide a way out of the impasse that kind of option embodies. But the few texts we have already brought to bear on the question make it sorely doubtful that James would have recognized in that pale term "right" the office of the passional for which he was arguing. For even if we eliminate the belief that "creates" the facts in some, not all, outcome cases, we are faced with too many texts where James is clearly making the claim that over-beliefs may actually *alter* the meaning we elicit from any array of facts we survey.[2] Over-beliefs, then, function in James's later thinking in much the same way as those "faiths" or "postulates of rationality" as make us more "sensitive to evidence" that bears in one direction rather than in another (DD 152; SR 89–92). Those phrases already suggest something stronger than a mere "right" to believe; James is clearly talking about a positive willingness or readiness to opt for one hypothesis rather than for its rival: a preferential inclination—if the term is not too pompous.

If all that is true, however, it would appear that James, both early and late, is proposing a view that is calculated to shock our epistemological sensibilities: the passional is being granted license to intervene *prior* to, and in a way that governs our intellectual survey of, the facts.

Notice how decisively this shifts the ground beneath the defenses of James's lecture we have been examining. Having equated outcome issues with *weltanschaulich* options, or at least ignored the difference between them, both Ducasse and Davis assume that the passional side of our nature may legitimately intervene in the settlement of any genuine option, but only *after* the theoretical survey of the facts has run out its string and come up dry, so to speak. But James talks frequently about our dealing with issues in such a way that the passional side of our nature does not, *in fact*, stand by until the theoretical intellect has exhausted its resources on the facts, and then cried "uncle." It is almost as though he had Ducasse and Davis in mind when he wrote that "The absurd abstraction of an intellect verbally formulating all its evidence and carefully estimating the probability thereof . . . is ideally as inept as it is actually impossible" (SR 92–93). "Pretend what we may, the whole man within us is at work when we form our philosophical opinions" (SR 92)—to which I would add, particularly when setting ourselves to those (*pace* Davis) "broad general themes" I have termed *weltanschaulich* issues.

Nor is it tenable to claim that one man's survey may be more dispassionate and objective and, because of precisely these qualities of mind, is more to be trusted than his rival's. James is boldly contending that *all* parties bring their differing "faiths or postulates" to bear on their survey of the facts. Even so zealous an upholder of scientific objectivity as Clifford is, like anyone else, whether he realizes it or not, "peculiarly sensitive" (SR 92), on passional grounds, to one sort of evidence rather than another. "Personal temperament," "mental temper" always make themselves felt in the ways different human beings "insist" that the universe speak to them, so that "Idealism will be chosen by a man of one emotional constitution, materialism by another" (SR 89). "Intellect, will, taste, and passion co-operate" in our forming of philosophical opinions of this sort, "just as they do in practical affairs" (SR 92);[3] that is the way of it, James insists, and the way of it for all of us.

It is, then, abundantly clear that the early James is arguing for a *pre*-intervention by the passional side of our nature, a guiding influence that temperament, emotional constitution, will, taste, passion, have it how you will, exert in the whole man's process of examining facts, selecting some as more significant than others, attributing larger importance to one group, lesser importance to another, and coming in the end to some settlement of the issue at hand. So, in "Reflex Action and Theism," having divided the mind into three "departments"—feeling (i.e., sensory perception), conception, and volition[4]—he lays it down that "The willing department . . . dominates both the conceiving department and the feeling department" (RA 114). He goes on to argue that theism is the most "rational" way— both practically and theoretically—of understanding our universe, and then concludes that "Our volitional nature must . . . , until the end of time, exert a constant pressure upon the other departments of the mind to induce them to function to theistic conclusions" (RA 127).

That same conviction that willing not only does but should dominate our sensory and intellectual functions is what James is plainly alluding to when he writes, in "The Will to Believe," of passional impulses which "run before" our beliefs, along with obviously less fortunate others which, bringing up the rear as it were, turn out to be "too late for the fair" (WB 11). This, then, is how we are meant to understand his claim that our passional nature may lie "at the root" of at least "certain" convictions we cling to (WB 4), as well as his diagnosis of the passional grounds on which we disbelieve a number of facts and theories while accepting others (WB 10). The same view pervades his account of our "feelings of duty" toward both truth and error as "only expressions of our passional life," an account that sets up the conclusion that two successive "first steps of passion" have committed those of his auditors who are still "with" him to adopt the epistemological canons he has been persuading them to favor (WB 18–19). The "previous" faith (WB 23), or "precursive" faith (WB 24), he shows as necessary by his three illustrations of "human" belief (WB 22–25) is meant to commend the legitimacy of "faith *running ahead* of scientific evidence" (WB 25; emphasis added).

Though the force of those expressions is somewhat weakened, for the purposes of my *overall* argument, by their frequent association with his questionable insistence that faith "creates" its own verification, they nonetheless betray unmistakably that in his own mind James is still working out of the conviction proclaimed in his other lectures: that our passional nature lies at the "root" of those faiths which work "precursively" on the conduct of our inquiry about a certain number of questions, at least— questions, I submit, which we are now entitled to identify as over-belief questions. James's original wording of WB 22–23 (given in *Works* 365n27.38) supports the same conclusion: when it comes to "goods" the "heart must lead" and not "follow" our knowledge, and the "passional nature dictate" our moral beliefs. WB 22–23 in its final form compresses to: "The question of having moral beliefs at all . . . is decided by our will," and "If your heart does not *want* a world of moral reality, your head will assuredly never make you believe in one." But the message is unambiguous; the insight Renouvier had supplied him at the crisis-moment of his life has borne fruit: our will can show its freedom by commanding the mind to sustain certain thoughts when other thoughts are possible to us, and when it comes to faith, that is what the will is precisely supposed to do. That insight, we have seen, is also vintage Pascal.

This placing of the passional *before* the cognitive was not, however, an idea James dreamed up to suit his purposes in "The Will to Believe" and in its companion essays; Perry shows that it was one of the earliest convictions to which James came during his study of the English empiricists—if, indeed, he did not already bring that conviction *to* his reading of them. They may not have inspired him to take his philosophical stand as an empiricist, but they surely confirmed him in his respect for "facts." And yet, he determinedly and consistently rejected every suggestion he found in them that the mind was some kind of passive spectator, to which the messages of sense knowledge merely came in from the outer world. In what Perry terms his "reform" of empiricism, one of James's crucial contributions was the claim that humans are creatures of "interests" *first*, and "knowers" only second. Desires, interests, "will" are the original prompters, directing the mind's active "reach" out toward reality. "In forming and trying hypotheses," Perry writes of James's "voluntaristic" form of empiricism, "the mind is not only active, but interested. It tries what it hopes is true. This subjective interest is both unavoidable and legitimate. If the mind wanted nothing, it would try nothing."[5]

That voluntaristic emphasis marks James's later thinking as well. For despite his subsequent regrets about the title of his essay, this precursive pressure in the interests of one over-belief over its competitors clearly represents a preference for, even a willingness to "go in for," the hypothesis to which our passional nature inclines us (SR 96). Even in his later correspondence, despite all his second thoughts, that precursive pressure is never denied, but repeatedly implied. The "will" to believe, he writes to J. Mark Baldwin in 1899, is " 'essentially a will of complacence, assent, encouragement, towards a belief already there,—not, of course, an *absolute* belief, but such beliefs as any of us have, strong inclinations to believe, but threatened' "; it is a " *'parti pris'* " which amounts to " 'the completest concrete expression of the individual's life,' " one that is operative in " 'all the great hypotheses of life.' "[6] Some two years later, he writes that his title had meant to designate " 'the state of mind of the man who finds an impulse in him toward a believing attitude, and who resolves not to quench it simply because doubts of its truth are possible.' "[7] No such human beliefs, James is convinced, can claim "absolute" status: they always remain reformable, since it is always possible that some array of future facts may argue for changing or even abandoning them. But even those future facts, James implies in his letters to Baldwin and Kallen, may legitimately be illuminated by a persisting over-belief that endows them still with a meaning or value consistent with itself, thus rendering that "threatened" over-belief stubbornly resistant to change. In cases like that, the over-belief could conceivably stiffen into the "strong inclination," the *parti pris* James talks about, or even into a posture of "resolve" facing up to an onslaught of hostile facts which threatens to quench it. But would we do justice to such a case by speaking about a mere "right" to believe—even a readiness, a willingness, to believe? Or could it be that the only honest term for such an attitude might be exactly what James called it: a "will" to believe?

The voluntaristic spine gives shape to James's thinking, therefore, from beginning to end. And yet, his teaching on the precursive pressure our passional nature exercises in the formation of our over-beliefs still remains open to two interpretations, of seriously unequal value. He wants us to conclude with him that human beings do, *as a matter of fact*, behave as he describes them: this pre-intervention of the passional is *de facto* the way of it for all of us. But

alongside this *de facto* conclusion, another possible interpretation of his argument suggests itself: that human beings *de jure* behave this way, that the pre-intervention of
the passional is always legitimate in settling issues of the
weltanschaulich sort. Now we experience a new surge of
sympathy for defenders like Ducasse and Davis, as well as
for the Millers and Cliffords against whom James was contending. For, taking the two interpretations jointly, one
might conclude that such pre-intervention is "legitimate,"
but by default, as it were; human beings not only *do* act
this way, but *cannot* (alas!) act otherwise, and that is the
end of it. The determinist's soup is the indeterminist's
poison, but both conclusions are at bottom matters of
incorrigible philosophic "taste"; and *de gustibus* . . .

Having placed the passional side of our nature, apparently at least, so much in command of the philosophic
process, James would seem to have opened himself wide to
the charge of legitimizing "wishful thinking," even if to
decide only a limited set of *weltanschaulich* issues. Indeed,
one must sympathize with those of his defenders who strive
to explain the intervention of the passional as occurring
only *after* the theoretical intellect has exhausted its efforts;
they are, at least, well-intentioned from a pro-Jamesian
point of view. And yet, if what I have argued to this point
accurately reflects what James said, it is not really James
his defenders wind up defending.[8] Can he still, in the context I have outlined, be defended from the "wishful thinking" charge?

Much has been said, in this connection, about James's
own temperamental aversion to credulity, as well as about
the audiences to whom he was addressing his remarks;
desiccation rather than credulity was what *they* needed
warning against![9] Valuable and apposite though these
biographical indications are, I am not sure they are always
couched in such terms as to get to the heart of the *philosophical* problem James has created. On that philosophical

problem, however, even in the context I have outlined, something may be said in his defense. The first line of that defense requires that we turn our attention to that, as yet, highly undiscriminated term: the passional side of our nature.

NOTES

1. For my reference to her "Pragmatism, Pragmaticism, and the Will to Believe," see above, chap. 1, note 1; see also James's letter to L. T. Hobhouse, written in August 1904, in *Letters* II 207–209.

2. Note that this view brings the term "facts" into closer resonance with the sense Smith explains as coherent with James's "radical empiricism" (*Spirit of American Philosophy*, pp. 47–49). This may attenuate the shock value of what James is proposing.

3. Note, however, the proximity of the temptation to make faith "create" facts, in this text and in its context.

4. See above, chap. 1, note 2, where it is pointed out that the same three "departments" are supposed in "The Will to Believe."

5. TC I 454, 455. Cf. 555–58, on James's reform of classical empiricism in the light of the same emphasis, and 570, on his approval of Leibniz' famous tag *nisi intellectus ipse*; see also TC II 79, on the role of willing in the association of ideas, and 258–59, on the priority of the moral will.

6. Given in TC II 243, 244.

7. Given in TC II 244–45.

8. Since composing the bulk of this essay, I find that Edward H. Madden, in his "Introduction" to *Works* (p. xi), expresses a view quite similar to the one articulated in this chapter: that intellect is, for James, *subordinate* to the affections, and that the willing aspect of life dominates both the conceiving and the perceiving aspects. There is, however, no suspicion of this view in his 1969 article (see Hare & Madden, "James, Miller, and Ducasse on the Ethics of Belief," cited in chap. 4, note 1); nor does he, in *Works*, either exploit this view or face the difficulties implied by it.

9. See, in this connection, William J. Macleod's "James's 'Will to Believe': Revisited," *Personalist*, 48 (1967), 149–66.

7

The Strata of the Passional

ONCE BROUGHT INTO FOCUS, the passional as James conceives of it seems at first to wriggle about like some living specimen under a microscope. It is initially striking to observe how many ways he has of designating that side of our nature. *The Principles of Psychology*[1] develops the argument that "belief," i.e., the attribution of reality to any item in the various "universes" we move in, from the flame of a candle to God, is always triggered by active "interest." We would not even notice, give our attention to, an object unless this active interest went before our act of noticing. Attention to *this* object already involves selecting *it* from out of a field of objects, attributing it importance. But how is this active interest to be described? James's response at this point is general and vague: in the field of everyday "practical" realities, an object even to be deemed "real" must "not only appear, but it must appear both *interesting and important*"; "*reality*," for objects in this "universe," "*means simply relation to our emotional and active life. . . . whatever excites and stimulates our interest is real*" (PP II 295). Similarly, to turn to the "universe" of sense realities: the "more practically important ones, the more permanent ones, and the more aesthetically apprehensible ones are selected from the mass, to be believed in most of all . . ." (PP II 305). A later summary has it that "Whichever represented objects give us sensations, especially interesting ones, or incite our motor impulses, or arouse our hate, desire, or fear, are real enough for us" (PP II 311).

Next, James turns to the universe of "objects of theory." Any theory, to be acceptable, "*must at least include the reality of the sensible objects in it*" and "explain" them satisfactorily. But more is needed: *"That theory will be most generally believed which, besides offering us objects able to account satisfactorily for our sensible experience, also offers those which are most interesting, those which appeal most urgently to our aesthetic, emotional, and active needs"* (PP II 312).

What we have in this final text is a formulation of the two levels of "rationality"—theoretical and practical— much as James outlines them in "The Sentiment of Rationality" (SR 75–82). In fact, he goes on immediately to quote an earlier form of that very essay, substantially identical with its final form; the quotation, and the entire essay as well, prompt us to look more closely at the summary phrase about "aesthetic, emotional, and active *needs*." For if all the features James means to include in the passional side of our nature—interest, practical importance, aesthetic apprehensibility, capacity to arouse motor impulses, or emotions of hate, desire, fear—come down to answering "needs," the specter of "wishful thinking" is indeed still with us. Our passional nature may induce us to believe in God, freedom, immortality, and the rest, as "realities" answering to our "needs," and James may be recommending that we believe, in the last analysis, whatever hypothesis in a genuine option we discover we most profoundly want to believe.

But James, as we have already seen, points out that, between one person and another, there are varieties of the passional nature: there are *different* "temperaments," "mental tempers," "emotional constitutions," and they guide the "whole man" in each of us to "insist upon being spoken to by the universe" in some particular key.[2] These differences in our individual passional natures, in other words, prod us toward different attributions of interest and importance, and therefore toward different over-beliefs. Not only are there optimists in the world, there are pessimists as well. And immediately an anomaly arises: one may accuse the optimist of wishful thinking, but the pessimist?

That question aside for the moment, James is making the same point in all these texts: our passional natures operate in each of us, and the results of that operation differ according to the tendencies they inscribe in us; hence, let no man claim he is that cosmic exception, pure mind operating in an emotional vacuum, with perfect detachment and objectivity. It would be less than fair to require James, while making this limited point, to reply to the next question that naturally occurs to us. But the question does occur, and inevitably so: Among these different passional natures, can it be claimed that some are more ideally constituted than others, more attuned to what *is* important in reality, such that their attributions of importance are more trustworthy than others?

We have already seen that Renouvier had proposed the view that all philosophic systems are, in the last resort, the creations of the individual philosopher's "temperament"; James, we know, made a note of this contention, and there is no doubt that it entered deeply into his own thinking. But where does this leave the question of deciding about the relative truth and adequacy of these various over-beliefs?

James frequently answers this question in a tag drawn from Cicero which he never tires of quoting and paraphrasing. There are, he claims, those who *vim naturae magis sentiunt*, who—by temperament perhaps?—are more clairvoyant than others on the inner workings of nature (SR 92), just as there are " 'philosophic constructions' " that are " 'more objective [than others] and cling closer to the temperament of nature itself. . . .' "[3] Some psychologists more than others are simply gifted with that " 'generous divination, and that superiority in virtue which was thought by Cicero to give a man the best insight into nature.' "[4] Baldwin had claimed "The Will to Believe"

amounted to a commendation of mere philosophical
" 'guessing' "; but the " 'guess' " involved, James replies,
may really be a kind of " ' "sympathetic divination," ' "
after all.[5] And Perry, summing up the very essence of
James, roundly affirms that "In metaphysics, as in human
relations, the chief source of illumination is sympathy."[6]
That view is profoundly Jamesian;[7] James stresses it in
"The Sentiment of Rationality": some men do have a
"superior sense of evidence," a "superior native sensitiveness" (SR 94). But such terms as "temperament," "native
sensitiveness," only bring up a further question: Are we
all predetermined to sympathize with whatever *Weltanschauung* we find consonant with our native endowment?
And does not that native endowment inevitably condition
us to believe that its sympathetic resonances, and no
others, "cling closer to the temperament of nature itself"?

To that conjoint question, when compelled to sharpen
the issue this way, James answers with a clear negative. It
is no surprise that he favors the "optimistic" endowment
over its opposite: but not any old optimism will do. In his
opening remarks in the lecture "Is Life Worth Living?"
he speaks with undisguised disdain of those "vulgarly
optimistic minds" and of the easy panaceas whereby your
"ordinary philistine feels his security" (SR 81).[8] If the
question were merely one of temperament, he goes on to
show, both optimist and pessimist would decide the question at issue in perfectly predictable fashion (LWL 33–
38).[9] He then devotes the remainder of his lecture to
breaking this log jam. For broken it can be, James is convinced, and the key insight for breaking it is that mere
temperament can be transcended: "even in the pessimistically-tending mind," he argues, there are "far deeper
forces . . . arousable," capable of bringing such a mind to
embrace the more correct optimistic view (LWL 47). Inborn temperament, therefore, may have the first, but need
not have the last, word. James goes on to claim that, when

properly addressed with the question whether life is worth living, temperaments may differ, but the "normally consti- tuted heart" will answer in "but one possible way," in the affirmative (LWL 50).

That shift in terminology is significant. The expression, with its suggestive echoes of Pascal's *coeur*, recalls one used in another essay: when faced with the question of morality in its widest *weltanschaulich* implications, James contends, it is our "total character," nothing less than our "personal aptitude or incapacity for the moral life," our "interior characters," that are being put to the test (MP 214–15). There is a difference between inborn tempera- ment and "heart," "interior character." Between the one and the other stretches the line of personal development.

We may have come a considerable distance from the understanding of our passional nature that is more regu- larly attributed to James, especially by his opponents. Ducasse, for example, speaks in this connection of such non-rational factors as "instinct," "impulse," or "tempera- ment," and, like others, accounts for James's personal solution to the God-question as congenial with his per- sonal "temperament." Perry, however, is more nuanced: the conclusions of his popular lectures do betray the "ardor of James's personal temperament," but other factors must be taken into account as well, among them his upbringing, and his earlier tendencies toward incredulity rather than its opposite; it would not naturally have occurred to him that critics would find him arguing for a credulity that was so directly counter to his native bent.[10] Perry's biograph- ical study, focusing on both the thought and the "char- acter" of James, invites us to look beyond questions of temperament and other features of his native endowment toward what James's life experience may have built upon those inborn qualities. There were, Perry sums up further on, not merely one but "four" William Jameses: the "neur- asthenic," the "radiant," and the James that was a blend of both. The "fourth James" was the living result of "experience and discipline—a transformation of native qualities into dispositions and habits." We must, Perry warns, take into account such growth-elements as entered into "the conscience of James, as distinguished from his native traits."[11] He quotes[12] in this connection a letter, dating from 1878, in which James defines "character" as "the particular mental or moral attitude in which, when it came upon him, [a man] felt himself most deeply and intensely active and alive. At such moments there is a voice inside which speaks and says: '*This* is the real me'!" James goes on to sketch the "attitude" of his own "real me" in terms that remind one forcefully of the attitude required by "The Will to Believe." He then makes a remarkable assertion: this mood he has tried vainly to describe "authenticates itself to me as the deepest principle of all active and theoretic determination which I possess . . ." (*Letters* I 199–200). It is not, he is suggesting, when we are playthings of our temperament, or victims of this or that mood-swing, that we are capable of our best "determinations," active or theoretic. That becomes possible in those times when the optimal synthesis occurs among all the factors of our psyche, inborn as well as achieved, and we are truly ourselves, really "in character."

Once more Perry's estimate is quite remarkably Jamesian. It recalls the famous chapter in *The Principles of Psychology* (PP I 104–27) in which James describes the process whereby this "transformation of native qualities into dispositions and habits" takes place. Especially interesting is the emphasis James lays on the development of what Bain had called " 'moral habits' "—a development which he envisages as molding the "plastic state" (PP I 127) typical of youth, through resolution, firm initiative, and continuous, consistent "[a]ttention and effort" (PP I 126), into that " 'completely fashioned will' " (PP I 125)[13] that he sums up as "character." "[B]y the age of thirty," he surmises, "the character has set like plaster, and will never soften again" (PP I 121). Whether or not that age limit be accepted, James's point is that whatever our native endowments and whatever the innate conservatism of our physiology, there is a plasticity in the human being amenable to "education," "acts of reason" (PP I 104), and the vigorous resolves of what Bahnsen had called the " 'moral will' " (PP I 124). The voluntaristic flavor of this entire discussion is vintage James; his excoriation of soft Rousseauan sentimentalism, his stress on "[k]eep[ing] the faculty of effort alive" (PP I 126; emphasis deleted) clearly presage his classic contrast between the "genial" or "easy-going" and the "serious" or "strenuous" moral moods. But especially suggestive for my present purpose is James's concluding paragraph of this chapter on habit: the development he is sketching results not only in a consistent power of moral action, but in a *"power of judging"* (PP I 127) as well. At first reading, it might seem that James is speaking only of the sort of judgment that makes certain men "the competent ones" in business, government, or like endeavors. But the context does not favor that restriction. James speaks of "whatever pursuits" a person may single out for his lifelong activity; he gives as examples the developments that lead to our becoming drunkards, "saints in the moral, and authorities and experts in the practical and scientific spheres." He implicitly equates all three examples, since for all the same law holds: we become what we finally become "by so many separate acts and hours of work," hours that see us "spinning our own fates, good or evil, and never to be undone" (PP I 127).

Here, I suggest, we are faced with another example of that "unconscious self-consistency" Perry finds so characteristic of James's thought, early and late.[14] His chapter on "Habit" reveals the same moralistic and voluntaristic emphases that run through all his philosophizing. In so doing, it provides a key, unlocking the riddle of the passional in the way, one may think, James's most alert thinking would have done it. The resulting understanding of the passional would imply that he is referring not merely to impulse, instinct, temperament, not merely to elements of native endowment, so varied in various individuals. He is asking us, rather, to expand our consideration to include the effects of education and the moral response to and active molding of our life experience which equip us in time with the "total character" we are, in part at least, personally responsible for fashioning as our own. A central feature of that total character will be, then, the "personal aptitude or incapacity for the moral life" we have come to attain; and crucial to that aptitude will be our developed power of judgment in moral matters.

We have seen that James himself does not explicitly discriminate the various factors in the passional nature to which he refers in "The Will to Believe"; nor does he discriminate the various appeals and pressures that go into creating an intellectual climate. He may well have thought those discriminations so obviously require that developed power of judgment that there was scarce need for going into both those questions in that lecture. In any event, the power of judgment he places at the terminus of character development does suggest itself as the instrument whereby both these discriminations could, and presumably would, be effected. The moral adult, one may assume, could as capably decide among the pulls of personal temperament, instinct, feeling, and the rest as among the fears, the prejudices, and the partisanships regnant in society's climate of opinion.

Now, it is just such a "moral" judgment James is asking us to make on the *weltanschaulich* issues that mainly concern us here; his claim is that the "normally constituted heart"—read: *properly* developed character—when rightly addressed with the question whether life is worth living, will, despite even a pessimistic temperament, "respond to fit appeals" (LWL 47) and answer in "but one possible way" (LWL 50).

How then should the question rightly be addressed? And what are these "fit appeals" that can be expected to solicit even the pessimistically-tending mind? James's answer invariably comes to this: when faced with the alternatives of living in the "genial," the "easy-going," or the "serious," the "strenuous," moral mood, the normally constituted heart, the person of character, will invariably choose to live in the serious or strenuous mood.

It can be objected that the attractiveness of the strenuous over the easy-going mood is simply a way of restating the appeal to our "aesthetic, emotional, and active needs"; "wishful thinking" has been set in a slightly different key, but the song is the same for all that. In fairness to the objector, too, it must be said that James gives frequent enough encouragement to that view. For he speaks more often of our "wanting" a world of moral reality (WB 23), of the "desire" for a certain kind of truth (WB 24), of our being "better off" if the religious hypothesis be true (WB 26). Elsewhere he claims that the religious hypothesis responds to a profound "craving of the heart" (LWL 40) by providing an "unseen spiritual order" which, if we "assume [it] on truth," may make "life . . . better worth living" (LWL 52). For it replies to our "highest interests" and most "vital needs" (LWL 54); it provides us with a world which does not baffle and disappoint "our dearest desires and most cherished powers" (SR 82). We have seen an analogous set of expressions earlier on, and they do, on the face of it, seem to open the door once again to "wishful thinking." But only, I suggest, on the face of it.

For the universe James summons us to believe in is strikingly different from the universe ordinarily associated with "wishful thinking"—so different, in fact, that the term would apply to it only in a grotesquely forced way. One would much more naturally speak of wishful thinking in connection with the sort of belief Perry terms the "comforting faith."[15] But, even when he is using the phrases quoted above, the faith James is urging us to adopt is a "fighting faith," the faith that invigorates the human capacity to respond to the often austere, even tragic, demands of living in the "strenuous" moral mood.

The belief in God to which he invites us does have its "comforting" quality, of course; but far more to the fore in James's mind is its demanding quality: belief in God grounds our active conviction that "there *is* a Spirit in things to which we owe allegiance, for whose sake we must keep up the serious mood" (LWL 43). "He who says 'life is real, life is earnest,' . . . gives a distinct definition to that mysteriousness [of things] by ascribing to it the right to claim from us the particular mood called seriousness,—which means the willingness to live with energy, though energy bring pain" (SR 86). Only the existence of some "divine consciousness," some "Infinite Claimant" can fully ground the sense of "*ought*" or "*obligation*" that a morality of the strenuous mood requires and imports; only on such a supposition does it make sense to say that " 'the universe' requires, exacts, or makes obligatory such or such an action . . ." (MP 192–96).

The capacity for this moral mood, James thinks, "probably lies slumbering in every man" but needs "the wilder passions to arouse it, the big fears, loves, and indignations; or else the deeply penetrating appeal of some one of the higher fidelities, like justice, truth, or freedom" (MP 211). But without God in the picture, the appeal to this sort of "moral energy falls short of its maximal stimulating power," for it "lacks the note of infinitude and mystery" (MP 212). With God in the picture, however, "the infinite perspective opens out" and the "scale" of the cosmic "symphony is incalculably prolonged. The more imperative ideals now begin to speak with an altogether new objectivity and significance, and to utter the penetrating, shattering, tragically challenging note of appeal" (MP 212–13), enabling the one who responds to it "joyously [to] face tragedy for an infinite demander's sake" and releasing in him every sort of "energy and endurance, of courage and capacity for handling life's evils" (MP 213). Only on such terms can we find assurance that our "bravery and patience" even in the face of the most "adverse life" is "bearing fruit somewhere in an unseen spiritual world" (LWL 57); that deeds of "faithfulness," "courage," "service," and "generosity" (LWL 59) make some ultimate difference; indeed, that "God himself . . . may draw vital strength and increase of very being from our fidelity" (LWL 61).

James's grounds for rejecting determinism are of the same moral sort: only a "moral universe" can claim from us this vigorous and exciting exercise of freedom, with all its possibilities of nobility as well as tragedy; the universe of determinism, however theoretically rational it seems, is "irrational in a deeper way," for it "violates [our] sense of moral reality through and through," so that we feel entitled to "deliberately refuse to keep on terms of loyalty" with it (DD 177). Only a universe in which our free acts truly count for something is of the sort that can require us to "live and die in its service" (DD 174).

This, I submit, is the imperious deontological background—entirely consistent with the moralistic voluntarism of his chapter on "Habit" and with its stern contempt for Rousseauan softness—that lends James's frequent eudaemonistic expressions their indispensable complement of meaning and force. Believing in God may be one way not merely of attaining our dearest wishes, but of "doing the universe the deepest service we can" (WB 28)[16] —the choice " 'involves a point of honor' " (LWL 50).[17] But our readiness, willingness, to believe in this sort of universe, James is convinced, is vitally bound up with our "personal aptitude . . . for the moral life," and with the developed power of judgment that permits us to perceive our world as soliciting our "allegiance," as having the "right to claim from us" the strenuous mood, and as disclosing the "Infinite Claimant" that alone fully grounds the sense of "ought" and "obligation" that strenuous mood imports. Not otherwise can we sensibly judge that " 'the universe' requires, exacts, or makes obligatory," or holds up for our commitment the "higher fidelities, like justice, truth, or freedom" for which humans may be expected to live with such austere, and often (apparently) unrewarded, qualities as "energy," "endurance," "courage," "bravery and patience," "service," "generosity," and "faithfulness," and in the end, as likely as not, be called upon "joyously [to] face tragedy for an infinite demander's sake." This is the martial James in Carlylean battle-dress, challenging us to share his lifelong romance with a world that persists in begetting heroes. " 'Hang yourself, brave Crillon! we fought at Arques, and you were not there' "— good King Henry, he is convinced, had the right of it (LWL 62).

There are, one must admit, distant echoes in all this of Kant's appeal to the sense of "duty," and of his proof for God's existence from "practical reason";[18] but those echoes turn out, on examination, to be only half the story. James remains obdurately Socratic, and Platonic, rather than Kantian. A Kantian purist would have to complain of this back-and-forth shift from deontological to eudaemonistic considerations, a shift largely responsible for the charge that James's thought-processes justify "wishful thinking." But neither Plato nor James will countenance the stark dichotomy between "duty" and "inclination," between what the "higher fidelities" sometimes austerely demand and what the rightly constituted heart most deeply yearns for. For both of them, if our cosmos is fully "moral," then the coincidence between eudaemonism and deontologism is forged in the developed moral agent who, in James's striking phrase, can genuinely *"want* a world of moral reality" (WB 23), want a world that makes stern, even tragic demands.[19] Not everyone, Socrates long ago implied, will judge that way: it takes "a man who is worth something" to focus, when his time comes, on that "one thing . . . whether he is acting rightly or wrongly, like a good man or a bad one," and take "no account of death or anything else, before dishonor."[20] But, temporarily ruled out of court, eudaemonistic considerations reclaim their rights the moment the moral judgment has been made: then Socrates can reassure his true "judges" that "nothing can harm a good man," not even this seemingly tragic condemnation to death; for "his fortunes are not a matter of indifference to the gods";[21] what has happened to him must be a "blessing" after all, and have come to pass not "mechanically" (ἀπὸ του αὐτομάτου)[22] but as it should, fairly, μετρίως.[23]

One is tempted to translate that μετρίως with the word "tunefully." It would be in deepest keeping with Plato's thought to imply that the gods "make music" with, and of, our checkered lives—a music only the "musical man" is properly attuned to, and can actively chime in with, in his living.[24] The metaphor, however, points back to what I suggest is one of James's happier illustrations of his own position; it is an illustration whose force is not always fully appreciated. Indeed, James himself may not have been alert to its full resources. He speaks of life as an "ethical symphony"; what he implies by that analogy is worth exploring. That exploration, though, will be the richer, and James's position placed in sharper relief, if we widen the investigation to all his illustrative metaphors on the topic of belief.

NOTES

1. Dooley ("Nature of Belief," cited in chap. 1, note 2), Roth ("Religious Philosophy of William James," cited in chap. 5, note 5), and Smith (*Spirit of American Philosophy*, cited in chap. 5, note 10) have already pointed to the importance of PP for the interpretation of WB and its associated lectures.

2. See above, pp. 85–87, and the passages quoted there.

3. Quoted in TC II 699–700.

4. Quoted in TC II 54.

5. Given in TC II 243–44; cf. I 24–26 and WB 27: our "passional" needs may be "prophetic and right."

6. TC II 704.

7. But it resonates with a longer and larger philosophic stream of thinking as well; see below, Epilogue.

8. I am quoting from SR 81, but in order to characterize the drift of James's argument on the same matter in LWL 33–34.

9. These pages should long ago have put to rest the idea that James's famous tag "it depends on the liver" was anything but what he terms it, a "newspaper joke."

10. Compare Ducasse, as quoted in Hare & Madden, "James, Miller, and Ducasse on the Ethics of Belief," 117, and Perry, in TC II 210–11, both of them focusing on WB.

11. TC II 701, 702; the entire section (699–704) is worth study.

12. TC II 699.

13. James is quoting John Stuart Mill.

14. TC I 449. It is not necessary, then, to think of James as consciously "remembering" what he said in PP when composing the lectures and essays being dealt with here; the consistency of one's personal philosophic orientation runs at deeper levels than that.

15. TC II 324.

16. I submit that Hick must ignore this deontological side of James in order to characterize his attitude toward the theistic alternative as "sporting," a "gambler's" attitude, with an eye on the "rewards" of faith and nothing more. But it must be said that even more sympathetic critics, like Roth, or Smith, come up well short of underlining its importance.

17. James is quoting Xenos Clark.

18. TC II 442.

19. This deontological flavor to what the "normally constituted heart" will "want," I suggest, is crucial to understanding the repeated term "ought" in the various faith-sorites James was later to construct (TC II 242–43). See above, chap. 3, note 6.

20. *Apology* 28B–D.
21. Ibid. 41C–D.
22. Ibid. 41D.
23. Ibid. 39B.
24. That metaphor, as I have tried to show elsewhere, later becomes the famous *carmen universitatis* figure which Augustine seems to have drawn from his readings in the *Enneads*; see my *St. Augustine's Early Theory of Man, A.D. 386–391* (Cambridge: The Belknap Press of Harvard University Press, 1968), pp. 170–71.

8

The Metaphors of Belief

SOME THINKERS are wary of metaphors, analogies; they class them with that semi-contemptible form of discourse the French dismiss with the phrase *c'est de la littérature, ça*. Cogency means technicity, and James's uninhibited reveling in metaphor they would ascribe to his "temperamental repugnance to the processes of exact thought."[1] Yet nothing contributes more to the full-blooded human appeal of his lectures than the zesty metaphors with which James flavors them.

At times his metaphors ensnare him, seduce him down pathways of development he might better have avoided. This may be especially true of the energetic, up-and-doing metaphors for which he had a predilection: in life, we are often very like an Alpine climber, staring at a terrifying crevasse, or like a train traveler suddenly confronted by a robber band. Dare, and you will do, shouts James, not from the sidelines, but from the midst of the fray. Your faith, if it has vital heat enough, will create the facts that will provide its verification. The fondness James had for such analogies may partially account for his defenders' tendency to think up other outcome illustrations to argue, misguidedly, I have tried to show, for the soundness of his views. It inveigled James himself, in less alert moments, to imagine that our ardent will could make it *be* true: the world *does* make sense, since our free moral activity *can* make a difference in the outcome of cosmic history. Almost, but never quite, he seems to insinuate that our belief, if strong enough, could even make it true that God *does* exist.

But those misguided uses should not blind us to appreciating the valid appeal these analogies had for James, or lead us to underestimate their "carry-over" value for his central thesis. The inclination to welcome, even to "want," a universe that both requires and rewards a life lived in the "strenuous" moral mood implies not only optimism and energy but plain "manliness" as well.[2] The further extensions of those analogies—their commendation of the faith which creates the facts of its own verification—he would have been far wiser to avoid. But the warrior's courage was, for him, very close to the heart of the matter. The fact is that none of his other metaphors for believing, despite their superiority in other respects, can quite convey this need for the "martial" spirit so congenial to the Jamesian heroic universe.

It may seem paradoxical but the metaphor that initially comes closest is a musical one. In "The Moral Philosopher and the Moral Life," he has brought his audience round to exploring the difference between the "strenuous" and the "easy-going" moral moods, and the need for a "God" to lend ultimate support to the "imperatives" proper to that strenuous mood. "Life, to be sure, is even in . . . a world [without God] a genuinely ethical symphony; but it is played in the compass of a couple of poor octaves, and the infinite scale of values fails to open up"; it "lacks the note of infinitude and mystery." But once believe that "God is there," says James, and "the infinite perspective opens out. The scale of the symphony is incalculably prolonged. The more imperative ideals now begin to . . . utter the penetrating, shattering, tragically challenging note of appeal," awakening the "stern joy" that leaps willingly to sacrificing life's lesser claims in response to the call of this "infinite and mysterious obligation from on high" (MP 212–13). The concomitant result—for eudaemonism is never totally absent from the picture—is that in this more challenging, even shattering universe, we derive from "the game of existence its keenest possibilities of zest" (MP 213).

The final metaphor I want to examine is drawn from the dynamics of personal friendship; we have noticed it already, since James employs it not once but twice in "The Will to Believe." He is comparing the critical attitude of a Clifford to the more open attitude of a readiness to "believe." The situation he proposes is that of a man "who in a company of gentlemen made no advances, asked a warrant for every concession, and believed no one's word without proof." Such a man, he submits, "would cut himself off by such churlishness from all the social rewards that a more trusting spirit would earn" (WB 28). James then makes the application to religious faith: shut yourself up in a Clifford-ish "snarling logicality, and try to make the gods extort [your] recognition willy-nilly, or not get [that recognition] at all," and you might well cut yourself off from your "only opportunity of making the gods' acquaintance" (WB 28). For we "feel," and (James implies) rightly feel, "as if the appeal of religion to us were made to our own active good-will, as if evidence might be forever withheld from us unless we met the hypothesis half-way" (WB 28).

James refers to this as a "trivial illustration" (WB 28) to support his argument for assuming a believing attitude in the religious sphere; but it is obviously, for him, something more than that. Just a few pages earlier (WB 22), he begins leading up to the appropriateness of "religious" belief by appealing to our sense that belief would be reasonable when it comes to deciding (*a*) moral questions and (*b*) "questions of personal relations." Whether "you like me or not," he observes in this latter connection, so often depends on "whether I meet you half-way, am willing to assume that you must like me, and show you trust and expectation." If either party "stand aloof, and refuse to budge an inch" until he or she "have objective evidence" that peremptorily *proves* affection is running in one or other direction, then the odds are that "liking never comes" (WB 23–24), and the rewards of liking and being liked are forever withheld.[3]

Allow me, for the moment, to prescind from the dominantly eudaemonistic cast of this illustration, as well as from its "will" (as against "willingness") to believe intentions; allow me, further, to fuse it with the later illustration in which the requirements of human friendship point to those that might govern our friendship with "the gods."[4] What then becomes plain is this: James envisages the dynamics of our friendship one with another as substantially parallel to those of our friendship with God.[5] In neither case is "objective evidence," of the Cliffordian sort, evidence that would "extort assent," available to us. But in neither case is the demand for such "objective evidence" an appropriate demand.

The demand for "proof" that "you like me," antecedent to my proffering any gesture to indicate my readiness to say "I like you," will (in the terms of the earlier illustration) almost infallibly ensure that "liking never comes" for either of us. It is in the very nature of the case that one of us, at least, show more "trust and expectation" than Clifford would allow us; indeed, it is far more probable that my decision that "I meet you half-way" will be the matching counterpart to my sympathetically divining your corresponding trust, expectation, and readiness to meet me that same "half-way." If, though (in the terms of the later illustration), one of us "made no advances, asked a warrant for every concession, and believed no one's word without proof," showed no "trusting spirit" toward the other, no sign of "active good-will," then the inception of a friendship relation is a chimeric hope—and, James implies, rightly so! Indeed, it could be argued, the person who would shut himself up in such "snarling logicality" would deservedly, by that very fact, "cut himself off" from the very possibility of friendship; to "demand," to insist, that friendship be "extorted" on these terms would be "churlish" at best, and at worst profoundly immoral.

The two appeals James makes to the dynamics of human friendship are, accordingly, perfectly parallel and easily fused—to this point, at least. We shall see in a moment that their application to the dynamics of religious belief is equally parallel. But there is a subtle difference between them, even on the human level.

The first example (aside from its bearing on the "will" to believe)[6] is set in a dominantly eudaemonist key. The demand for "objective evidence," in this case, precludes an outcome I may dearly "desire," an outcome James likens to the "promotions, boons, appointments" the general run of mankind hopes for. The stress is on the fact that my untrusting attitude results in my inevitably losing all the rewards, joys, consolations, of friendship; my attitude, accordingly, is both unproductive and unprofitable.

The second illustration sounds a distinctively deontological note. It rings forth, at first, in a typical Jamesian Victorianism: the demand for objective evidence is simple "churlishness," unbefitting the "company of gentlemen." Even, James would have admitted, were it to redound to my profit and advantage, were this conceivable as happening in an interpersonal relationship, it would still be vulgar, low, "ungentlemanly." The proper attitude among cultivated humans requires "our making willing advances," exacts the exercise of "our sympathetic nature," the farthest thing from the determination to "extort" affection from the other "willy-nilly," as it were. Only the "trusting spirit," James concludes (in the eudaemonistic key again), may expect to "earn" all the "social rewards" that grace the life of "gentlemen" and elude the grasp of the churl.

Again, in this treatment of the interpersonal relationship I have smuggled in expressions James employs in that other relationship—of man to God—he hopes to illumine.[7] This was meant to emphasize the fact that *both* illustrations of the interpersonal are substantially interchangeable, correspond to and complement each other, and parallel point for point the man–God "friendship" relation James is focally discussing.

Now I should like to suggest that there is, between these two types of Jamesian illustration—life's "ethical symphony" and the appropriate overtures of friendship—a set of kinship features that makes them both more exquisitely shaped than perhaps even James imagined for pointing to the dynamics, and appropriateness, of the "believing" attitude. They are, in significant respects, supremely better fitted to that task than illustrations of the Alpinist or truck-driver sort—and this despite the fact that they are, in their own way, outcome cases.

First, there is in both cases the question of an option; I may decide to make that first sincere, and risky, overture of friendship, or retreat back into my shell. But the same is true in the symphony example: I may on first hearing find Bach or Beethoven too demanding, off-putting, even alienating, and choose to turn the dial to the more accessible comforts of some popular crooner.

The option involved in both cases can, furthermore, be live, forced, and momentous—surely not on the same scale as the God option, but on a certain level of importance, nonetheless. Consider first the friendship example. It can be a live option for me to risk making this friend, no difficulty there. But the situation can be such that this option is also, in all human likelihood, existentially forced; an occasion may have presented itself, with this particular person, which risks being unique, a now-or-never possibility—all the more so since I may sense that a negative response on my part can very well ensure that I may never be able to count on a similar opportunity. And the choice between a friendship and the sterile loneliness of leaving a certain corner of the heart forever untenanted may be (and in all too many cases is) more momentous than many of us acknowledge.

But the symphony example manifests, in its own way, those same three features. Imagine that some occasion has awakened the realization that I might well develop an interest in the music of Beethoven. Until that moment my musical world has been limited to popular tunes, and I have been quite comfortable in that familiar, relatively undemanding range of enjoyments. An initial exposure to Beethoven has confronted me with musical possibilities that are inviting, but at the same time ominously forbidding. His symphonies attract as richer and broader than the "couple of poor octaves" that nourished me until now; and yet, his intimations of "infinitude and mystery," his "penetrating, shattering, tragically challenging note of appeal" have something unsettling about them. The choice between resting complacently with what I already know and relish and making the strenuous ascent toward the "stern joy" of those stormy musical heights represents a choice between two live alternatives. The option could, in its way, also be existentially forced; I cannot know whether I shall ever in the future be so seriously tempted, find the entry into this difficult world so invitingly paved as now; I cannot be sure, but I can sense it as a strong likelihood that this chance will never come again; the "no" I say now may be a "no" either for my entire lifetime or at least for an important part of it. And I am led uneasily to suspect that something truly significant will be missing from my life if I do say "no." There is a quality of the momentous in my option now.

It is at this point that some defenders of James would inquire whether their ambiguity criterion is satisfied by these two cases. Yes, and no: more importantly no than yes. For while these are, in their own way, outcome cases, they are markedly different from the outcome cases like that of the Alpinist or the streetcar passenger: they are far more parallel to the *weltanschaulich* type of question in which, I have contended, James is mainly interested, and to which the most benign interpretation of his essay applies.

The first difference from the usual outcome type of case is this: there are no "facts" of a truly experimental sort that could be appealed to as "verifying" in advance one alternative as preferable. "Hindsight" verification fares slightly better, but even *after* opting for this friendship, or for an active immersion in Beethoven's world, what observable facts could I conceivably adduce to "show" another that he or she should choose the same or any similar option? I can plead (in the eudaemonistic key) that "having chosen this option, I have found the quality of my life immensely enhanced"; but then I am asking for "belief" from my opposite number, and for a "believing commitment" to the course I have taken. Nor will a mere "experimental" commitment do the trick. One has to "give" oneself in friendship before friendship can really come to flower; and though it is not so manifest in the symphony example, a similar self-commitment is the very condition for taking Beethoven's universe seriously enough to reap its "rewards."

Suppose, though, I couch my appeal in a more deontological register. There are various considerations I could invoke to persuade my interlocutor that the "churlish" self-isolation James finds so humanly unacceptable—so "ungentlemanly"—is something stronger than that: it is a refusal to respond to and honor the personal value embodied in the other, a way of treating the other as just an item of furniture in my depersonalized world, and so it is a subhuman, even anti-human, attitude that is profoundly immoral. But my recalcitrant acquaintance could very well respond that I have begged the question; for his wait-

and-see attitude exactly prevents him from "seeing" such a personal value in the potential friend, and therefore grounds his refusal to expose himself to the only experience that might shake and perhaps eventually reshape that attitude. His form of misanthropy will, indeed, persuade him that the "experience" I claim to have had, both of the (eudaemonist) rewards and the (deontological) value claims of "readiness" toward friendship, along with every human poem and story on the same theme, are merely so many futile records of uncritical credulity and romantic self-delusion. And substantially parallel considerations could apply to my efforts to solicit his making any "willing advances," bringing an "active good-will," to the experience of Beethoven's world.

A further feature of these two examples is this: they are far more appropriate for illustrating the "pre-intervention" of the passional side of our nature for which James, in his most alert thinking, was arguing. For the kind of option being called for is one which the purely "theoretical" man could never be brought to make on coldly evidential grounds. To stay with that example for the moment: the decision to risk a friendship calls for, not some objective survey of facts—"he smiled at me" or "his handshake was warm and firm"—but a sympathetic weighing of facts which amounts to a receptive appreciation of those facts as signs: "that was the sincere smile of a good man" or "one can trust a man who shakes hands like that." To arrive at such interpretations of "facts," readiness and general trustfulness, a dropping of the skeptical guard, a willingness to go "half-way"—all the phrases James applies to our gaining the friendship of "the gods"—must "go before" or, more exactly, interfuse with, our intellectual appreciation of what we have experienced. Even more exactly, perhaps, our "experience" itself will be the resultant not only of what the potential friend has said or done, but of how the passional side of our nature influences our interpretation of what our friend's sayings, doings, even silences are to import for us.

It should be noted, in justice to Clifford and Miller, that one can, in such cases, be totally uncritical, credulous to the point where ardor of heart induces softness of head. One can, on the one hand, so "wish," so yield to the need and desire, to make a friend and enjoy the rewards of friendship that the "will to believe" short-circuits one's questions about whether this person *is* the sort of person of whom one *should* want, can realistically hope, to make a friend. The immoderate "will" to believe can easily deprive us of sound judgment, making us dupes for the other's cynical manipulations. Or, on the other hand, the "will to believe" can bring on that anxious, spastic kind of "over-trying" that snuffs out the possibility of a serious relationship the moment the other divines its presence. But objections of this sort only serve to bring out another vital difference between these two cases and the cases Ducasse and Davis propose. The energetic, muscular "will" to believe does not even occur to the mind when dealing with friendship or the sympathetic entry into a world of art. When dealing with the "churl" in his misanthropic self-enclosure, James occasionally speaks as though the "will" to believe could "create its own verification" even in such cases. But his more alert language betrays the fact that he is truly dealing with an "openness," a "readiness," toward assuming a "believing spirit." Indeed, one has only to conjure up the scenario of the voluntarist's "making" a friend or "enjoying" Beethoven by the same sheer effort of will that goes into leaping an Alpine gorge, and the notion is worthy of Molière. All this would appear to argue, once again, that James was largely correct in eventually repudiating the "will" to believe, and might have been better advised to speak consistently of a "willingness" or "readiness" to believe from the very outset. No

"will" to make a friend ever succeeded in "creating the
facts" serving as its own verification. But no friendship
was ever joined without some willingness to believe.

When it comes to friendship, then, the will to believe
differs from the willingness to believe, and the crucial difference is a matter of developed "judgment." But under-
lying the judgment is, among other things, a respect, even
a reverence, for the other. It refuses to extort, but invites
and holds itself in readiness to welcome and respond to, the
other's free self-disclosure. Once that self-disclosure is
granted, though, it is seen as laying a claim on reciprocal
disclosure, a claim that demands new respect. Only out of
such respect can the "rewards" of friendship spring; again,
the deontological and the eudaemonistic go hand in hand.
But the manner, timing, and pace of growing response is
always a matter of judgment, sensitivity.

Those terms, so often applied in aesthetics, hint again
at the kinship between this and James's "symphonic" illustration. Few catch-phrases have been accorded more
delusory force than the notorious *de gustibus non est dis-
putandum*. "I know what I like," says the tourist, con-
temptuously turning his back on the *Mona Lisa*: my
"taste" is what it is, and has the same *droit de cité* as anyone else's! But varieties of this kind of spontaneous, un-
tutored "taste" are much like the varieties of temperament,
native endowment, and inborn passional nature that James
invites us precisely to *evaluate*. That they are various does
not *eo ipso* warrant the conclusion that they are all on the
same footing; indeed, it raises the very question whether
they *can* be. Can it really be that they all cling just as
closely to the "temperament" of great art? Scarcely; and
immediately various avenues present themselves toward
the expansion, refinement, cultivation of spontaneous
taste. The "education" of artistic taste imposes, in its way,
the same task of personal development, the same "attention," series of "efforts," "hours of work"—in a word,

much the same resolute asceticism—as James prescribes
for that refinement of our inborn endowment which results
in the man of moral "character" and concomitant soundness of moral judgment. Plato's "musical man" is not
merely born; a certain native endowment may be necessary
to him, but then he must actively consent to "become" the
fully musical man for which his native gifts initially fit
him. Only then is his *developed* taste, his ripened "judgment" about matters musical, to be trusted. Only a man
comparably musical, furthermore, will be capable of appreciating the soundness of that judgment—and even then
only if he consents to allow a measure of receptive sympathy, sensitivity, and willingness to "run before," or,
better, *interfuse* with, his critical activity. A new-found
world of music, like a potential friend, invites us to meet
it "half-way." And—what is too little attended to—not
only do both sorts of invitation promise enjoyments as yet
unexperienced, they lay certain claims on us, make demands—on our "willing suspension of unbelief," our
readiness to lend a patient, respectful, and receptive ear,
to go *into* it, heart and soul.

And so, James rightly insists, does the "moral universe."
In any of the *weltanschaulich* issues that absorb his central
interest, or, rather, in that connected web of issues that
all come down, for him, to the single question of whether or
not we live in a moral universe, it is not cold "fact," or any
assemblage of "facts," that ever closes the debate for one
side or the other; it is always a question of how we "experience" the very same facts as others experience, how we
weigh them, what importance we accord them. Ducasse
was persuaded that the evils of our world made the God-
hypothesis, for him, a dead option. For James, he admits,
those evils took on a different "weight"; but he then too
readily dismisses the difference as a matter of "temperament."

But there was, I have tried to argue, more than temperament, impulse, or instinct at work, both in James's personal development and in his most alert thinking. One does not expect an adult to attach so much weight to a headache or toothache as a child will, and even children are some more namby-pamby about such matters than others. But how much weight should the adult attach to the cancers, injustices, cruelties, and catastrophes, the whole array of evils Ducasse *chooses* to denominate "gratuitous"? Individual evaluations will differ. But can James truly be faulted for pointing out that the meaning and importance we attach to the obstacles, resistances, even horrors, of our common experience, will depend in significant measure on our fiber, resilience, courage—in short, our developed capacity for the moral life lived in the strenuous mood? How much "right" we accord the universe to lay such austere claims upon us depends, in crucial measure, on the reverence—what Dewey calls the "natural piety"— we choose to bring to our "experience" of that universe. And the Jamesian decision to believe in our universe as "moral," in our lives with all their admixture of torment and gladness as "worth living," and when all is said, to believe in God as Infinite Claimant, is in the last resort less a matter for "debate" than a question of "judgment."

Only a person experienced in genuine friendship, in its demands as well as its rewards, is equipped to avoid both the uncritical credulity and churlish standoffishness that preclude friendship's ever happening. Only the musical man will bring to hearing a new symphony not only the eagerness to enjoy, but the suitable respect for a work of art and the chastity of demand that goes with developed musical judgment. And if there is any merit to the generous understanding I have tried to elicit from his thought, James's most fundamental contention comes down to saying something quite parallel about *weltanschaulich* questions. If we do indeed inhabit a moral universe, it is in the very nature of the case that only a person of developed moral sensitivity, sympathy, and "judgment" will be sufficiently attuned to discern that truth. Only such a person will have the requisite readiness and willingness to "experience" that side of the great human option as more rewarding than its opposite, and, even more than that, the side on which life enlists our loyalties, not despite, but even because of, its sometimes "shattering demands."

But there is risk in wagering on this side of the great human option; fearful risk. The crevasse may be too broad for leaping, and the robbers destined to inherit the earth. Not one to solve the mystery of evil by blinking it away, James stared it straight in the eye, and guessed at the dread possibilities he saw there. We bet against those possibilities in the coin of our entire selves. "It is only by risking our persons from one hour to another that we live at all," and the Alpinist must display the "wisdom and courage" to "believe" he can make the leap (LWL 59). If life is really a "fight," and with all its "sweat and blood and tragedy" it certainly "*feels* like a real fight" (LWL 61), then Wordsworth's lines are apposite: we need " 'the virtue to exist by faith / As soldiers live by courage' " (LWL 60).

It is striking to observe how often James links faith with courage, and how regularly that linkage summons up the martial metaphor. Three times in his popular lectures he appeals to the Alpinist's quandary, and the linkage is evoked each time; the same thing occurs with the scenario of the robber band. Predicaments like these, he never tires of reminding us, put a premium not only on optimism, energy, and decisiveness, but also, and especially, on courage. "[R]ecklessness may be a vice in soldiers," he admits, but it does not follow that "courage ought never to be preached to them": the "courage weighted with responsibility—such courage as the Nelsons and Washingtons never failed to show."[8]

This, he contends, is the kind of courage he has been

preaching in all his commendations of faith; for when all is said, James sees faith as "in fact the same moral quality which we call courage in practical affairs" (SR 90); or, to quote his friend William Salter, " 'as the essence of courage is to stake one's life on a possibility, so the essence of faith is to believe that the possibility exists' " (LWL 62).

But faith need not always come garbed in martial dress. Hence, the appropriateness of the friendship metaphor: it points up the readiness and willingness that go into the formation of many of our over-beliefs—a readiness and willingness that quite suffice under the calm skies of most of our days. The symphonic metaphor, especially when surging toward its "penetrating, shattering, tragically challenging" climax, transports us from cloudless skies into the swirling dark of life's stormiest moments.

But the Alpinist faces his terrible decision at the very eye of the storm, and the robber band confronts us with life at its most menacing. Moments like these may be rarer, but when they come they assault us with gales of hostile fact which threaten to rip into tatters every optimistic over-belief that flew so bravely through our fair weather days. Did James have such moments consciously in mind when he wrote of the need for a threatened over-belief to stiffen on occasion into a "strong inclination," a *parti pris,*" a positive "resolve"? Perhaps not consciously; and yet, the case he has made for belief, when stripped of its flaws and taken at the top of its strength, entitles our making that connection, and warrants our speaking of a genuine "will" to believe, after all. For the Jamesian universe, if we accept it, is "earnest infinitely." Shot through with ambiguities, it plays us down to our bottom card. That bottom card, to win, must show naked manly courage.

Rather than indulge our want and weakness by conceding us the right to believe, the Jamesian universe imperiously summons us to grow up, until strong enough and self-forgetful, we bravely decide to trust in, and resolutely collaborate with, its often inscrutable ways. Only the most curious definition of terms would warrant our labeling that response "wishful thinking."

NOTES

1. The phrase is Perry's, from TC ii 680.

2. Perhaps I should apologize for the term, but the Greek word for the sort of "courage" I mean is, after all, ἀνδρεία. It was the typical soldier's virtue, and James's fondness for military metaphors is a matter of record. I am afraid that "personliness" will not quite do here.

3. James goes on to speak of the "desire" to know one is liked, of the "promotions, boons, appointments" that come to him who believes he can attain them, and so acts that his belief "creates its own verification." He is, again, working in the context of an outcome situation, where "will," as against "right" or "readiness" to believe, may in instances "create its own verification." I am taking the liberty here of shifting the thrust of his illustration, applying it to the "right" or "readiness" to believe, but with the encouragement (or warrant?) accorded by the analogous interpersonal illustration he uses only slightly further on in this same essay. My purpose at this stage has become more philosophical than scholarly.

4. Again, in hopes of bringing forward the fullest merit of James's argument (a philosophical question) I am giving it the most benign interpretation that his text will bear.

5. This raises the question, in my mind at least, whether James can so readily dispense with a "personal" God as his earlier characterization of "religion" might seem to imply: cf. WB 25–26.

6. See note 3, above.

7. See notes 3 and 4, above, on my purpose in this.

8. William James, *The Will to Believe and Other Essays in Popular Philosophy* (New York: Dover Publications, 1956), p. xi.

Epilogue

On Becoming Humanly Wise

There are flaws and missteps in James's justification of "The Will to Believe." The content analysis presented in my first chapter tries not to hide those flaws; on the contrary, I have attempted so to present James's argument that the reader will later recognize the points at which critics have directed their fire, while at the same time highlighting a set of features which eventually argues in James's defense.

It would, however, be impetuous for the reader of James's lecture to dismiss it out of hand by pointing to James's ebullient manner, his sporting metaphors, or his congenital impatience with the ways of exact technical thought: my first step (Chapter 2) in defending James took the form of showing how profoundly serious he always was about such *weltanschaulich* questions as the religious hypothesis. The Wager argument, and the capital John Hick made of it in his damning critique of James's lecture, suggested probing James's relationship with Pascal and with his celebrated "reasons of the heart" (Chapter 3). Again, James's seriousness receives confirmation, for his debt to Pascal may have been larger than he consciously recognized; it may, in fact, have been his lifelong familiarity with the *Pensées* which sensitized him to the decisive influence Renouvier's fideistic thought was to exert upon him at the crisis-moment of his young life.

But difficulties with his lecture still remain. Can James be acquitted, for instance, of the charge of commending "wishful thinking"? My fourth chapter presented both the objection and a series of responses Jamesian defenders have proposed to answer it. Both objectors and defenders, though, share a number of common assumptions which, once explicitly stated, reveal themselves as questionable. They assume, first off, that the "will" to believe can be evaluated by excogitating outcome cases of a streetcar or truck-driver sort; my fifth chapter tried to show that James, on the contrary, was primarily concerned with over-beliefs, even while his own appeal to outcome illustrations introduced elements of confusion into his main argument. Chief among those confusions is his talk of faith's "creating" the facts of its own verification, as though such faith truly bears on *weltanschaulich* issues.

But James himself later encouraged us to regard that kind of fact-creating faith as ultimately irrelevant to over-belief decisions. Discard it we did, and passed on to explore a second assumption: that he entitled the passional side of our nature to intervene only *after* the intellectual side had done its dispassionate work, and failed to resolve matters. My sixth chapter presented evidence to show that James, both early and late, clung consciously and tenaciously to the contrary view: our passional natures not only do but must exert a precursive influence on all our cognitive activities, and quite especially in resolving those *weltanschaulich* questions in which the facts themselves are essentially, not merely accidentally, ambiguous.

Does this Jamesian contention reduce all our *weltanschaulich* options to products of our passional nature, and plunge us once again into the morass of "wishful thinking"? There are passages, one has to admit (Chapter 7), in which James seems to give countenance to that view: our philosophies could well be intellectual constructs eudaemonistically chosen because of their consonance with our inborn temperaments, and with the wants and interests corresponding to those temperaments. But the passional, for James, is a more articulated entity than that: not only are there temperamental differences from one individual to another, but each individual boasts other strata of the passional besides temperament. In his alertest thinking, James brings us to consider the voluntary labor of education and habit formation whereby we mold these inborn endowments into fully-formed "character," with its capacity for moral judgment; this is what is put to the test in over-belief decisions. Central to any rightly formed character, moreover, James contends, is the freely developed capacity for making those ultimate choices not simply at the behest of our temperamental wants and interests, but in the "strenuous" moral mood—a mood which, synthesizing eudaemonism and deontologism, makes us actually "want" a world that makes austere, sometimes even shattering, demands on the slumbering hero dwelling in each of us.

This robust streak of deontologism has, generally speaking, been little noticed by James's loyal defenders; it is almost as though they thought it an embarrassment better passed over in silence. But without it James's defense of belief falls into a shambles, and the sinew goes out of his view of the universe. How typical, for instance, his way of settling the argument between optimist and pessimist: he wastes no time arguing that our eudaemonistic cup is half-full rather than half-empty; he goes straight for the deontological jugular, to arouse those "wilder passions" that fuel response to "higher fidelities" like justice, truth, or freedom. "Stop your snivelling," one can almost hear him scold, and "get to WORK like men."

That indispensable deontological stress is both final testimony to his seriousness about matters of religious belief, as well as the feature of his thought which effectively silences the charge of "wishful thinking." In concert with the eudaemonism that James refuses to divorce from it, that deontologism subtly threads its way through, and lends coherence to, those two key metaphors he proposes to illuminate the dynamics of belief: the friendship and symphonic metaphors. But the Jamesian universe requires him to put forward, at the end, a stronger metaphor than either of those. The evils of our universe are as menacing and real as any robber band; the crevasses we must leap might terrify the hardiest Alpinist. Friendships and symphonies may illustrate justification for a "right," a "willingness," even a preferential "readiness," to believe. Those more tempered attitudes serve us well in normal times. But risk, danger, evil call for a sterner attitude: despite his own later demurrals, I submit that James was not all that misguided in originally arguing that there are features and moments in human life which challenge us to stiffen our "willingness" into a genuine "will" to believe. Clarify its fundamental intentions, and straighten out its occasional missteps, and that argument can still take hold on minds and hearts today—and, one hopes, for a thousand tomorrows.

But James should not be considered a lone voice crying in the philosophic wilderness. His links with Renouvier and Pascal are relatively clear, but he speaks for a distinguished tradition that runs longer and more broadly than those two forebears. It is suggestive, in fact, how often Western philosophy has found itself compelled by the developments of its history to take the turn James proposes, and proclaim the revenge of that forgotten truth: that the pursuit of wisdom inexorably grips the whole human being, not merely brain and mind, but heart, emotions, imagination, and sensibility as well. This is the fact of the matter, and James is surely right to remind us of that much. The most solemn warnings against our allowing the passional side of our nature to intrude upon the search for human wisdom are themselves dictated by that passional nature, speaking in one of its moods, and a one-sided mood at that. That mood comes down, as James trenchantly puts it, to one of timidity: we are advised so to dread making mistakes that we slink away from where the fighting is at its thickest, most testing, and at the same time most decisive. Is life worth living? Are we free, and do our human actions really count toward the issue of the cosmic struggle into which we have been plunged? Does there exist an Infinite Claimant who urges us to live in the "strenuous" moral mood? Such questions have lain at the center of humankind's concern since the dawn of reflection; and yet, our generals would order us to take our seats at the outer edges of the struggle, and endlessly sharpen the weapons of epistemological objectivity which, the history of thought has proven over and over again, never come up to the challenge that *weltanschaulich* questions throw down to us.

Banish subjectivity, and an entire spectrum of questions drifts out of philosophy's range—the very questions about which humankind most sorely needs, and is called upon most peremptorily, to take sides. Abstain from taking sides until every tiniest epistemological scruple has been put to rest, and you have, without acknowledging it, taken sides already. For the claim to have banished subjectivity is an illusory claim; subjectivity still skulks in the wings, whispering its cues, but now in their most desiccating tones. The only honest solution lies in recognizing the ineradicable influence subjectivity wields in human thought, confronting it squarely, and educating it for the role it will play, openly or secretly, as long as humans are human.[1]

This Plato saw clearly when he wrote of a Republic in which the whole of the soul—mind, passions, and bodily appetites—would be disciplined, enchanted, and harmonized not only by exercise in thinking, but by music and myth and daily familiarity with noble and beauteous forms. He feared, and rightly, the bloodless mind that reduced philosophical exploration to the kind of clever logic-chopping young people can be taught to do so facilely, and fancy themselves paragons of wisdom in doing it. Philosophizing must be concerned with truth, evidence, and argument, Plato saw, but never reduced to that concern. For the mysterious visage of Being radiates more than truth: it shines out as Goodness and Beauty as well; the true shepherd of Being has to be educated to yearn for Goodness, and, most important, to respond with "reverence and awe" to the sometimes tragic demands of Justice and Piety, Beauty and Nobility. Only such a fully developed human being can grow out of egotism, surmount credulity, and then be trusted to philosophize with the interests of the wider human community at heart.

Something very like this evaluation of the philosopher's task, one may think, lay behind Aristotle's reluctance to teach philosophy to the young: they lack the "experience" that furnishes the truly ripe materials for responsible ethical pondering, but the experience that also seasons and matures the one pondering as well. Only the morally wise can decipher the demands of moral wisdom, much as the properly sensitized spectator is alone attuned to catch the solemn cadences of tragic drama.

Those ancients thought of philosophy as a way of life, an art of living wisely, responsive to the fullness of Being's riddling self-revelations. So for the Stoics, Plotinus, and Augustine, philosophy and spirituality coalesced into the single task of producing human beings worthy of the title "wise," seekers, lovers, and "musicians" all in one. Only such a fully ripened human being, they were persuaded, can look with an artist's practiced eye at the evils of our universe, and be large enough in spirit to assent that it is "good, very good"—good, and hauntingly beautiful, a *carmen universitatis*. Aquinas brought the message forward with his emphasis on the power of "knowledge by connaturality," that sympathetic conformation to the "temperament of nature" itself, and writes an extended treatise on how the "passions" of the soul both might and must be tempered and refined to play their proper role of resonating with Being in all its rich variety.

Descartes rang in the modern epoch by accusing will and passions of unlawful entry into the philosophic mansion; with him, and with the rise of modern science, we have witnessed the triumph of that passionless, "objective" spectator, pure reason. Kant showed in turn how little that pure reason could confidently pronounce upon the central questions that decide the hopes and ideals of mankind, but now epistemology took up its reign, a solitary eminence presiding over a desert landscape from which feelings, emotions, and passions had been peremptorily banished. There might be more things in life than were dreamed of by this philosophy, but the philosopher was sternly warned to keep them for dreaming hours only, at least until this passionless mind could minister to the myopia it brought to its own inspection of them. Being, for this critical mind's eye, shrank down to "the true"; only the "certain" was of any valid interest, along with the canons of evidence and argument the mind kept sharpening, sharpening to hunt that elusive quarry. Subjectivity was equated with subjectivism; passionate thinking was always dangerous. The intruder must be kept at bay, or exiled to alien fields like poetry, literature, and religion: suspect exercises in self-indulgence on which the philosopher must glare with baleful eye, if indeed he glance at them at all. That Orpheus figure, the passionate thinker, was replaced by the ascetic and slightly anemic schoolmaster, the academic philosopher.

Pascal protested: the "god of the philosophers" had no heart. Johann Fichte protested mightily: this tyranny of the epistemological sapped the human being of all the energy required to fulfill the moral "Vocation of Man."[2] Nietzsche protested: the Apollonian had throttled the Dionysiac, and humans no longer learned to dance. The Romantic poets flooded the world with protests: the rainbow was more than an optical equation, and skylarks more than ornithological specimens. The din became more deaf-

ening, but our desiccated devotee of certitude answered
it by mounting higher in his lonely tower where, in reedy
voices, he and his companions talked of logic, and analysis, and the shoddy tricks that poets played with their un-
scientific abuses of language. Soon, nobody else was
listening.

But now the din is being raised in other quarters. The
very ones most trusted to hold aloft the banner of passionless objectivity are proving disloyal; Michael Polanyi,
Jacob Bronowski, Thomas Kuhn are bruiting it about that,
whatever "routine" scientists might think, imagination,
aesthetic sensibility, all the juices of the "personal" and
passion-laden, do indeed run through the veins of every
creative scientist. Not so surprising, after all, Dewey would
have commented: for wasn't science itself, at bottom, a
form of "art"?

Philosophers themselves, we are now being told, must
abandon their obsessive concern with the search for epistemological "foundations," and take their marching orders
from the pragmatism of James and Dewey. The quest for a
foundational philosophy has proven futile; we must recognize that there is "no method of knowing *when* one has
reached the truth," give up our "hope of getting things
right," and content ourselves with "clinging together
against the dark." Philosophizing is simply an unending
"Socratic conversation," but "We are not conversing because we have a goal," the discovery of truth.[3]

The quandary that inspires this counsel of despair is
very real; but everything we have seen in this study indicates that the solution is far from Jamesian.[4] For nothing
could be clearer than James's passionate conviction that
in claiming that we *are* free, that life *is* worth living, and
that our belief in God's existence is closer to the truth
than its opposite number, he had "gotten it right." But he
came to those convictions precisely by adopting an epistemological "rule" that the entire drift of post-Cartesian

philosophy would call into question: that taking the risks
involved in arriving at the truth is a sounder way of approaching these questions than succumbing to the fear of
error. This obliged, and therefore (he felt) entitled, him
deliberately to invite the passional side of human nature
to enter as an ingredient in the very process of philosophizing, to think, not as dispassionate mind, but as total
human being. He knew full well the fears others had expressed about the passional, but he saw them as stemming
from an undiscriminated notion of that side of our nature.
Think "passional," and you must think wildness, uncon-
trol, anarchy, egotistic self-indulgence, subjectivism, relativism, wishful thinking at its least responsible—in short,
the "chaos come again" that his friend Dickinson Miller
deplored. Think "passional," in other words, and frequently the last thing it suggests is the synonym that James
proposed for it at its educated best: "character." Yet that
was his hope for, and trust in, the passional side of our
nature which the universe itself endows us with, surely not
out of sheer malevolence. That hope he shared with Plato,
Aquinas, and even (in certain of his moods at least) Nietzsche: that the passional can be tamed, controlled, actually
rendered clairvoyant; that it can be not only governed but
invited into the very citadel of governance, bringing with
it the fire that fuels the total human response to Being in
all its facets.

But that hope, that project for development of the passional, suggests how James might have replied to the counsel of despair alluded to above: that it issued from the very
spirit of desiccated inquiry, obsession with "method,"
which prompted the despair in the first place. Instead of
following that counsel, we must turn, instead, or perhaps
return, to educating complete human beings rather than
bloodless minds. The philosopher may reply that his function is a limited one: that literature and the arts are better
designed for the tasks of developing the lively yet chas-

tened sensibility, the leaping imagination, the ripened life of feeling, emotion, passion, which must be trusted to contribute to, rather than intrude upon, the human task of reading the temperament of nature. This, the philosopher may protest, is not our "job," not our "professional responsibility." That, I suggest, James would consider an abdication. For to be a genuine philosopher is more than a job, more than a profession: James, one has to speculate, would have thought it, as Fichte did, more a vocation. In answering to that vocation, the philosopher must answer from the fullness of a mature humanity: he must embody, in himself and in his manner of philosophizing, the synthesis not only of respect for facts and careful exactitude in reasoning about them, but of sensibility also, of imagination, feeling, and passion—the synthesis he hopes his students may, each in their individual mode, eventually replicate.

No single philosopher can ever claim to fit that description perfectly. But in significant ways the portrait resembles James: and this, I submit, is why young students, budding philosophers as they natively are before we manage to thin out their blood, feel they can trust the judgments of a man who obviously succeeded in becoming and remaining so thoroughly human. For this is the test that, in the end, sane human beings inevitably apply to their mentors: are they, too, sane and fully human? Have they made the acquaintance of reality in all its exuberant richness, not only accurately but sensitively, analyzing, yes, but musing and pondering as well, even dreaming; ocsionally, perhaps, as Plato intimated, praying? The educated judgment of one attuned this way to nature's temperament may not always get it *exactly* right. But still, James would reply, sanity urges us to judge that such a person cannot be too far off the mark. At very least, he or she will provide us with something that has enough of the solid ring of reality about it to ground the largest choices life commands that we make, and does not permit us indefinitely to postpone.

That, I submit, is the most we can ask of any human thinker. It is still a great deal. Not only will it have to do; it will do.

NOTES

1. "It is utterly hopeless," James writes in SR 92, "to try to exorcise such sensitiveness by calling it the disturbing subjective factor, and branding it as the root of all evil. 'Subjective' be it called! and 'disturbing' to those whom it foils! But if it helps those who, as Cicero says, 'vim naturae magis sentiunt,' it is good and not evil."

2. After reading a preliminary draft of this study, Professor John Lachs suggested that a probe into James's philosophical relationship to Fichte could shed important light on the development of his thought. I cannot but agree: the resonances with Fichte's *The Vocation of Man* ringing throughout these popular lectures seem to me, as to Lachs, unmistakable.

3. See Richard Rorty, "Pragmatism, Relativism, and Irrationalism," *Proceedings and Addresses of the American Philosophical Association*, 53, No. 6 (August 1980), 719–38, esp. 724, 726–27, and 734 for the quotations cited here. Rorty's full-scale study *Philosophy and the Mirror of Nature* (Princeton: Princeton University Press, 1979) fleshes out the argument for the same conclusions. There is much in both of Rorty's contributions with which I find myself in sympathy, but they do not win him the right to cloak his disaffection toward "getting things right" with a Jamesian mantle.

4. In WB, for instance, after as withering a critique of the various foundational "tests" for truth as Rorty's own (pp. 14–17), James goes on to say: "But please observe, now, that when as empiricists we give up the doctrine of objective certitude, we do not thereby give up the quest or hope of truth itself. We still pin our faith on its existence, and still believe that we gain an ever better position towards it . . ." (WB 17).

Appendix A

"The Will to Believe" and James's "Deontological Streak"

After publishing the preceding study of James's classic lecture under the title *William James on the Courage to Believe*, I was grateful to the reviewers who dealt with it, for the most part, with such kindness. This was especially so because I had over the years developed such an admiring fondness for that lecture.

But it came as no surprise that even the more receptive reviewers did not conceal that they had honest reservations on one point or another.[1] Those reservations, significantly, instead of flying like arrows aimed at haphazard and landing all over the target, zeroed in for the most part on several points of convergence. Was I, my critics asked first of all, correct in speaking of James's ethics as revealing a "deontological streak"? And if so, did that deontological lean persuade James, perhaps only half-aware, to justify the precursive influence of "will" on the formation of our *weltanschaulich* "over-beliefs" in a way that turns out to have been far more voluntaristic than genuinely "pragmatic"? In the light of that last objection, finally, have I, when all is said, succeeded only in exposing (in both senses of the term) James's defense of belief as viciously circular?

In this essay I mean to confine myself to the questions centering about the existence of that "deontological streak." But because several of the issues already men-

An earlier version of this essay appeared in *Transactions of the Charles S. Peirce Society*, 28 (1992), 809–31.

tioned, including that of deontology, have since been given a keener edge by the publication of James C. S. Wernham's study *James's Will-to-Believe Doctrine: A Heretical View*,[2] a few introductory observations on Wernham's book are in order. I shall restrict myself to the issues which figure into the discussion of James's "deontological streak."

A DIFFERENCE IN PURPOSES

And, first, it should be noted from the outset that Wernham's object in writing his book was markedly different from mine. I made no secret of my twin convictions that, first, James seemed to be making an important cluster of philosophical points in his *Will to Believe* and in the whole series of "popular" lectures which form its "setting"; but that, second, he did not always succeed in making those points as cogently as they deserve to be made. I set myself the task, accordingly, of striving to sift out what was valid in James's intentions, and then improving his argument until it was cogent enough to drive home the point he had hoped to make. Wernham, for his part, is content (as he has every right to be, of course) to examine James's argumentation exactly as it stands, then decide on what conclusion (or conclusions) that argumentation gives him the right to draw.

It is not entirely clear that Wernham clearly grasped this difference between our approaches: he contends, for instance, that James's logic authorizes him to conclude only that we are "better off" if we choose to "bet" on God's existence. But "betting," Wernham argues, is not necessarily the same as "believing" that God exists. This is the context in which he makes his only allusion to my study (p. 119*n*12): he appears to class me with those (like John Hick) who look on betting as necessarily an unserious business, and therefore unworthy of consideration when it comes to taking a stand on the religious question.

A bet, Wernham rightly points out, can sometimes be a deeply serious undertaking.

A closer reading might have shown him that on the page he cites I was arguing precisely against John Hick's contention that James was recommending we bet on God's existence, and that he could have meant that term "wager" only in the relatively frivolous, "sporting life" understanding of the term. Far from disagreeing with Wernham, I hoped to make it clear that there were un-questionably elements of the "serious" kind of bet in what James was recommending. The Jamesian universe, I wrote in concluding my study, is "earnest infinitely" and "plays us down to our bottom card. That bottom card, to win, must show naked manly courage."[3] (p. 121). Surely that is betting language, but (*pace* Hick) the language of a profoundly serious bet!

But does this mean that I think James would have been happy at being told that his argumentation authorized us to "bet" on God's existence, but not to "believe" that He existed? Not in the least. For it may be true, as Wernham reasons, that one can bet on a horse without necessarily believing that the horse will win (pp. 103–105), but I can-not accept that James's commendation that we choose to "believe" in God's existence was meant to be of the same quality, weight, and seriousness as the advice of a tout, however soberly given, that we wager on Number Six in the Third. Had James read Wernham's book, and been convinced by it, I imagine him wanting to go back to his own essay in hopes of beefing up its reasoning so that it wound up warranting the stronger conclusion he had originally hoped his readers would feel entitled to draw.

To repeat, though, Wernham's conclusion seems per-fectly consonant with the intention commanding his essay and the method entailed by it: that of carefully ana-lyzing what James's argument *actually* warrants as its conclusion, and permitting him no stronger a conclusion than his argument *genuinely* warrants. This is one valu-able task the philosopher can choose to take on, once he has become aware of the gaps and difficulties in James's essay. I, on the other hand, chose to take on a different task, one more like the one I imagine James might have taken on: that of closing the gaps and ironing out the difficulties, out of the conviction that the essay's original conclusion was sound enough and important enough to merit salvaging.

THE PRECURSIVE INFLUENCE OF THE "PASSIONAL"

Whether or not it should be viewed as a gap or difficulty, my own study of James's essay convinced me of a feature which few if any defenders of James seemed to have noticed: I have called it the "precursive influence of the passional." It does not appear that Wernham himself has noticed this feature or dealt with the devastating objection it could be made to represent to James's entire argument. I have to think it quite remarkable that none of the reviewers chose to challenge the central claim which, I had thought, was the most revolutionary feature in my interpretation. Briefly put: I found that James was arguing not only that the "passional side" of our nature did intervene in the formation of "belief" *after* our intellectual survey of the evidence had come up dry, so to speak, but also that it presided (and legitimately) before and during, influencing and even commanding, that intellectual survey.

Patrick Dooley, however, objected to that claim (p. 575), but from an unexpected quarter: he wondered why I considered it in any way "news." He and (so he claimed) three authors before him had stressed that for James, both early and late, "passional demands tremendously influence both our beliefs and overbeliefs."[3] Whatever justice there may be in Dooley's contention, it seemed clear that the message he and his colleagues had striven to convey had not gotten through to a spate of writers—Kennedy, Hick, Davis, Muyskens, Hare, and Madden (in an earlier article)—who had focused their studies precisely on this famous lecture, and, whether

attacking or defending James, wrote as though our passional side might intervene only *after* an intellectual survey of the evidence had left us still in doubt. Besides,
half reluctantly admitting the precursive influence of the
passional may be one thing, facing it squarely and satisfactorily resolving the difficulties it entails is quite another. And that, *pace* Dooley, I found nobody doing—
not, at least, to my satisfaction.

But Dooley's ostensible agreement with my contention
soon turns out to veil a deeper disagreement; he finds my
way of interpreting the *force* of this precursive influence
profoundly unpalatable. For he sees, and rightly, that my
interpretation threatens to elide, indeed, to positively exclude, the step of verifying the truth of our over-arching
"beliefs" by means of any "pragmatic check" (p. 574).
Dooley's fear is well-grounded, for my claim comes down
precisely to this: if my interpretation of James's "will"
to believe is correct, then when it comes to our truly
weltanschaulich beliefs, all such pragmatic verification
can have only the remotest relevance, so that appeals to
such verification come to little more than a charade.

For, as James describes it, the influence which the passional side of our nature exerts on our intellectual survey
of the evidence is, and indeed *should* be, sufficiently powerful to *guarantee* that, in deciding *weltanschaulich* questions like theism *vs.* atheism, freedom *vs.* determinism,
pluralism *vs.* monism, we shall come to a truly sane and
healthy conclusion. Now, this view of how the passional
intervenes pulls the teeth out of any pragmatic verification of theism; for what can "verification" genuinely
mean when the will has foreordained the conclusion that
our observation and reasoning must come to?

But this certainly seems, at first glance anyway, to in-
dict James of holding a voluntarist position in which the
responsible weighing of evidence on either side of any
"belief" question no longer counts for anything: that, in
a nutshell, is the difficulty regarded more from the epistemological point of view. Another way of putting the matter, though, is this: placing the passional side of our

nature so much in control of the formation of our beliefs would seem to make James guilty of the charge so often leveled at him: the charge of "wishful thinking." This is the same difficulty as we saw above, but expressed, now, in more ethical terms: James is giving us a license to believe whatever we find it attractive to believe.

I am convinced that whichever framing of this difficulty the pro-Jamesian defense attorney chooses to deal with, he will eventually be compelled to make an appeal to the "deontological streak" in James's moral-religious thinking. Permit me, though, to leave the epistemological side of the difficulty for treatment on some future occasion; allow me to restrict myself here to showing how it is important, for answering the "wishful thinking" charge, to recognize the existence of a "deontological streak" in James's ethical thinking.

THE "NON-PRECURSIVE" INTERPRETATION OF JAMES

It is not difficult to understand why a number of critics have accused James, in "The Will to Believe," of defending our right to "wishful thinking." Wernham's study illustrates, albeit unintentionally, the conception of James's argument which lays it open to this charge, even if one assumes (as most writers do) that the passional side of our natures does *not* exert its influence precursively. On that assumption, James would imagine our thinking about the theistic hypothesis (to take that example) as normally running this way: we start by making as dispassionate a survey as is humanly possible of the evidence and reasons on either side of the issue; suppose, now, that after this intellectual evaluation both negative and positive conclusions make an equal appeal to our intellects: the issue, in other words, is undecidable on intellectual grounds. Suppose, further, that we cannot indefinitely postpone making some decision; we must decide one way or the other. In such a case, this school of writers say, it is legitimate to allow the "passional" or "willing" side of our nature to decide the issue on the basis of which alternative appears more desirable than its competitor.

This seems to be the scenario Wernham is implicitly following when he writes (p. 103) that it would be foolish "not to gamble on theism . . . because an 'immediate reward' . . . attaches to the act itself of betting on that side. That reward," Wernham goes on to explain, "James called 'the strenuous mood.' The capacity for it could be activated, he thought, by postulating theism, not just by believing it; and the strenuous life was the best life whether or not it was the right life."[5]

The Entry of "Wishful Thinking"

Now, there are several features of Wernham's case here which I must temporarily ignore in order to go straight to the point I intend to deal with. But the fact that I pass over them without demurral should not imply that I agree, for instance, that James seriously intended to argue only that we may "gamble" on theism, or that activating the "strenuous mood" requires only that we "postulate," not that we "believe" in, God's existence. But my differences with Wernham on both those points undoubtedly derive from the basic difference between our intentions, as I tried to explain above. The point that interests me here, though, concerns Wernham's appreciation of what James means by the "strenuous mood," and how he sees it fitting into James's argument for the will to believe.

From the language used above, Wernham looks on living in the "strenuous mood" as the "immediate reward" (he borrows the term from Ducasse) "attaching to the act itself of betting on that [i.e., the theistic] side." This language seems to imply that for the willing or passional side of our nature to opt for theism, we must be attracted by something in the nature of a "reward." This, in turn, is consonant with Wernham's position that the kind of choice James is summoning us to make is a "prudential" one, by which Wernham means that we choose that which will make us "better off" (pp. 15–16, 20). Wernham has, in short, made the "strenuous mood" function as a motivating object in what he calls the "prudential" type of decision. Further, by making life in the "strenuous mood" more *desirable*, he has made it the kind of life we would naturally "wish for"—and by the same token made "wishful thinking" the crucial motor in our decision to believe.

The "Genial" and "Strenuous" Moral Moods

I have, in my essay, consistently used the term "eudaemonistic" for what Wernham calls "prudential," and I see no difficulty in accepting his specification that such a prudential/eudaemonistic decision always turns on what promises to make us "happier" or "better off." Both of us, moreover, set the prudential type of decision in contradistinction to what Wernham calls the "moral," and what I prefer to call the "deontological," type of decision. And we would both concur, unless I mistake him, in characterizing this latter sort of decision as turning on what we perceive as "obligatory," irrespective of whether doing it promises to make us "better off" or not.

Now, it is common knowledge that James divides the human universe into two main classes or ethical types. Those in the first and perhaps the more common type tend as a rule to make their ethical choices in eudaemonistic or prudential terms, looking to what will leave them "better off": these James labels as living in the "genial" or "easy-going" moral mood. The other, rarer type is more inclined to make certain of its ethical choices, at least, in what I have called deontological and Wernham calls "moral" terms: they are far more sensitive than their easy-going counterparts to the inspirational power of the honorable, the noble, the heroic, even (and perhaps especially) when the summons to a course of action makes self-sacrificial demands on them. These are the tenants of what James calls the "strenuous" moral mood.

Now, James would undoubtedly admit that most of the routine decisions of life can legitimately be made in accord with the "genial" calculus of what leaves us "better off." But he also insists that there are moments and situations in life in which our human mettle is tested by our capacity to put "better off" considerations in a remote second place, and decide in accord with the canons native to the "strenuous" moral mood. To express this in the terms I used above, eudaemonism is an ethic which will serve quite adequately for our fair weather decisions; James would have no difficulty admitting this. But he was also convinced that life can turn stormy and suddenly make austere demands upon our capacity for the heroic; then, he insisted, the genuinely moral person must be able to shift ethical gears and respond to challenges in the "strenuous" moral mood. Now, this is the type of ethical attitude I tried to characterize when I spoke of James himself as possessing a "deontological streak."

The "Strenuous" or "Serious" Moral Mood

Two of my critics raised direct questions about that interpretation; Tilley (p. 755) found my "claim to have uncovered" such a streak "debatable," while McDermott complained that one would never guess from what I had written that James was a "consequentialist" in ethics. No wonder, then, he found my use of the term deontologism "unfortunate": surely, he hoped, I did not mean to "equate James's position with the bleak, situation-free deontological ethics of Kant and H. D. Ross"? In analyzing James's use of the "friendship" metaphor, moreover, I had suggested that the term "willingness" to meet the other half-way was more appropriate than "will," but the dynamics of that metaphor did not strike McDermott as "in any way deontological" (p. 190). That second observation is at least half-right, but it should be clear from my text that James's appeal to the friendship metaphor warranted only a limited conclusion: the deontological emphasis, I argued, emerges far more appropriately from the "Alpinist" and "robber-band" metaphors James *also* brings to bear. I cannot resist remarking here, however, that analysis of the stages in a growing friendship might well reveal a deontological *side* to that process and that James, I think, would have been sympathetic to that suggestion.

In any event, I carefully forbore from characterizing James's ethic as *purely* deontological; the expression I used was that his ethic had a "deontological streak." Hence, I may waive the necessity of comparing him at any length with either Kant or Ross: those gentlemen I leave to take care of themselves. But I am questioning the adequacy of McDermott's characterization of James's ethics as "consequentialist," in any pure sense of that term. Madden's remarks (in *Works* VI, pp. xxxi–xxxii) provide a lead toward my contention: "James's moral philosophy," he writes, "is clearly teleological and utilitarian," but he "clearly diverges from classical utilitarians" by transforming their "pleasure" into the broader "satisfaction of needs, wants, and desires." But, Madden goes on to say, "In addition, there is an active and volitional, even heroic, dimension to value experiences to which utilitarianism, James thought, does not do justice." He had no use for a world in which "there was no genuine evil to overcome and hence no heroic gestures and sacrifices needed. He preached the gospel of Thomas Carlyle and Rudyard Kipling when the mood was on," despite the danger that preaching involved, of embracing the "notion that evil can be considered instrumentally good."

That was not the only paradox James was flirting with, but let it pass for the moment; it is Madden's recognition of the "heroic" motif in James's ethics that is worth dwelling on. One of James's clearest statements of his difference from classic utilitarianism occurs in the early essay "The Moral Philosopher and the Moral Life" (pp. 142–45) which James himself, Madden avers, considered the "most important one" in the volume containing "The Will to Believe." But the "addition" it brings to his already modified form of utilitarianism goes somewhat further, I suggest, than Madden allows: it shows that James perceived that all "eudaemonisms," all forms of "consequentialism," were inadequate as ethical theories unless they admitted the balancing complement of the "deontological streak" I claimed to find in him.

He commends the "Benthams, Mills, and the Bains" on their lasting service in tracing so many of our ethical ideals to their "association with acts of simple bodily pleasure and reliefs from pain." Their form of eudaemonism, accordingly, James would accord a wide field of applicability, as I pointed out earlier. But, James goes on to say, "it is surely impossible to explain all our sentiments and preferences in this simple way." The sentiments he refers to include a "vast number of our moral perceptions" which "deal with directly felt fitnesses between things, and often fly in the teeth of all the prepossessions of habit and presumptions of utility." Consider, for example, the "sense for abstract justice which some people have" or the "feeling of the inward dignity of certain spiritual attitudes, as peace, serenity, simplicity, veracity." Such value judgments are, he contends,

quite inexplicable except by an innate preference of the more ideal attitude for its own pure sake. The nobler thing *tastes* better, and that is all that we can say. 'Experience' of consequences may truly teach us what things are *wicked*, but what have consequences to do with what is *mean* and *vulgar*?

But the robust sense in which James is using terms like "taste," "mean," and "vulgar" becomes clear from the second of two illustrative examples he gives. What if

the hypothesis were offered us of a world in which Messr. Fourier's and Bellamy's and Morris's utopias should all be outdone, and millions kept permanently happy on the one simple condition that a certain lost soul on the far-off edge of things should lead a life of lonely torture, what except a specific and independent sort of emotion can it be which would make us immediately feel, even though

an impulse arose within us to clutch at the happiness so
offered, how hideous a thing would be its enjoyment when
deliberately accepted as the fruit of such a bargain?

This passage, I submit, illustrates perfectly what I
meant by James's "deontological streak." He does not
deny that experience of "consequences" can and does in
numerous cases serve as our criterion for what is ethically good or bad; but he insists that there are other cases
where a different criterion must be acknowledged—a criterion which not only complements, but would actually
correct the kind of decision we might otherwise make on
purely consequentialist grounds.

James goes on to "applaud the intuitionist school" (the
Kantians, presumably) for having perceived this side of
the matter. But his true forebears, I still suggest, lie further back, in thinkers like Socrates and Plato, who saw
that there were cases in life when we need to apply such
categories as James here appeals to: the "noble," the
"ideal," the "inward dignity" of certain acts and attitudes
for their own "pure sake." But all such appeals, I suggest,
invoke a deontological intuition, an insight into simple
"oughtness."

This side of James's ethics never effaces the "teleological" (what I termed "eudaemonist") side, any more than
Plato's "deontological streak" effaced his own basic eudaemonism. In both thinkers, rather, it complements, and
on occasion corrects, the force that eudaemonistic criteria would otherwise exert too unilaterally on the basis of
foreseen desirable consequences.

In my essay (pp. 101–104), I presented a number of
examples instancing the Jamesian language of deontologism;[6] he talks of owing "allegiance" to a "Spirit in
things . . . , for whose sake we must keep up the serious
mood," of a "mysteriousness" in reality to which we ascribe "the right to claim from us" the mood of "seriousness, . . . the willingness to live with energy, though
energy bring pain"; he speaks of God as the only "Infinite
Claimant" who can adequately ground the sense of

"ought" and "obligation" the strenuous mood imports and exacts from us. For with God in the cosmic picture the "more imperative ideals . . . speak with an altogether new objectivity and significance, . . . utter the penetrating, shattering, challenging note of appeal," the appeal, even, "joyously [to] face tragedy for an infinite demander's sake."

Most of the texts above, though not all, come from "The Moral Philosopher and the Moral Life," that "popular lecture" which I take to be the close companion of "The Will to Believe." Texts like these could be multiplied; but even these few indicate why I cannot agree with Madden's characterization of that essay (*Works* VI, p. xxx) as a "classic example of a teleological system *as opposed to* a deontological one" (emphasis added). Teleological it is, yes, or, as I would prefer to term it, eudaemonist (for surely *both* eudaemonism and deontologism can adopt teleological form),[7] but a eudaemonist system large and comprehensive enough to accommodate the unmistakable deontological "streak" I speak of: for the Jamesian universe (as another of his popular lectures asks us to believe)[8] holds out the hope that our acts of "bravery and patience" in the teeth of the most "adverse" kind of life may, despite everything, bear "fruit somewhere in the unseen spiritual world." Our universe, in other words, may sometimes make heroic demands on us, demands whose "consequences" *we* cannot see as other than simply "tragic"; and yet, James was convinced, our deontological fidelity may be—no, *must* be—eudaemonistically teleological in the cosmic long run.

Texts like these, accordingly, convey the "taste," or the moral "intuition" if you will, which impelled James, from one end of his career to the other, to prefer the "strenuous" as "more ideal" than the "easy-going" moral mood, and consequently inspired his lofty regard for human "heroism." But they also suggest why his famous "ladder of faith," in its non-logical way,[9] would naturally run from the high value he placed on life lived heroically in the strenuous mood, to his passionate belief that our universe must ultimately be hospitable to that type of moral existence. That kind of "match," after all, between the universe and the human creatures it has brought forth, contains nothing self-contradictory; it *might* be true, *may* be, is *fit* to be true. To this point the faith-ladder is moving in the eudaemonist mood, the mood of the "desirable."

But now his argument shifts into the "imperatives" much more coherent with deontology: it *ought* to be true, *must* be true. If eudaemonism were the governing consideration, the last step would issue into a "wish" or "right" to believe; only the injection of deontology can account for James's much more robust conclusion, "It *shall* be true, at any rate for *me*." That, I submit, is unmistakably the language of voluntarism, of nothing weaker than a resolute "will" to believe.

This is why I argued that, despite his later vacillations and even demurrals, James was correct in concluding that we "ought," in certain circumstances, exert a positive "will" to believe. But, my argument ran, those circumstances were of the kind which demanded of us a deontologically motivated resolve to live or continue living in the "strenuous" moral mood *despite* the evil "consequences" such a resolve appeared to entail. For the universe can sometimes require us to believe in what "outstrips the evidence," that some heroic-tragic act we are called upon to perform will, after all, bear fruit "somewhere in the unseen spiritual world." And it is especially in such circumstances that the universe requires that we grit our ethical teeth and "will" to believe, at the same time as it affords us an occasion for the noblest type of moral accomplishment of which humans are capable.

But notice that acts like these must be performed far more out of regard for those "higher, more penetrating ideals" which the Jamesian "intuitionist" advocates than out of any foresight of "rewards" or satisfying "consequences." Indeed, the "preference of the more ideal attitude for its own pure sake" comes far closer to uttering a categorical "let the consequences be damned." For that reason, I submit that James would have found it distinctly odd of Wernham to classify living in the strenuous mood as itself a species of "reward" for believing in, or postulating, God's existence. That whole style of thinking seems as intrusively alien to the strenuous mood as it would be to insert a harmonica solo into Beethoven's "Eroica" symphony.

One may feel free to question whether this explanation succeeds in "salvaging" the philosophical truth implicated in what I called James's "most alert" teaching; one may feel equally free to question the solidity of the view I have presented, Jamesian or not. But there is one possible accusation I shall never understand: that (*pace* John Hick) any such act of spiritual bravery can fairly be mistaken for that pallid child of the "easy-going" moral mood, "wishful thinking."

WERNHAM AND WISHFUL THINKING

But I submit that even if we were to sanction Wernham's manner of inserting the "strenuous mood" into James's argument, it would lay that argument wide open to the wishful thinking charge. For in the ordinary meaning of the term, wish becomes father to our thought when we are contemplating the prospect of being happier, more comfortable, and satisfied: "better off," in Wernham's phrase. Think of the "strenuous mood" uniquely or primarily in terms of "reward," and the wish for that reward can skew our thinking toward adopting the conclusion which ensures our receiving that reward.

But the universe of the "strenuous mood" is traversed by dangers and evils which generate shattering and even tragic ethical demands: does one naturally and spontaneously think of that as the kind of universe one would "wish" for? Even James, when speaking of the heroic type who would "want" a world of this stern sort of moral reality, is clearly using the word "want" in a more muscular sense than we normally accord to the term "wish."

This is why I attributed such importance to the "deontological streak" in James's ethic; especially after claiming
that the passional side of our natures exercised a precursive influence on our intellectual processes, James's argument sorely needed that relatively disinterested ethical
attitude to save the decision for theism from the self-
indulgence of wishful thinking.

DEONTOLOGY IN *VARIETIES OF RELIGIOUS EXPERIENCE*

Once it is granted, however, that the deontological streak
is prominent in James's earlier "popular lectures," the
question arises whether that accent persists through his
later works. For it could be true that the deontological
motif may be vital to the understanding of his essay on
the "will to believe" and still represent an aberrant theme,
one not truly "Jamesian" in the most authentic sense. It
is undeniable, for example, that the opening sections of
Varieties of Religious Experience, written some five years
later,[10] seem to downplay the "volitional" moment in religious conversion, subordinating it to a passive surrender
which normally implies giving up one's own will and acquiescing in the will of the unseen higher powers.

Yet even in these pages the religious attitude resembles
the "strenuous mood" in several respects: it always imports a "*serious* state of mind," a certain "gravity." It is
"hostile to heavy grumbling and complaint," is "solemn,
serious" (pp. 38–39), "accepts the universe" even with its
evils, "heartily and altogether." But there are differences
as well: it seems to transcend the purely moralistic type
of strenuous mood in that the "service of the highest is
never felt as a yoke" to be shouldered with cold and
heavy heart. There is a tremendous difference, James
holds, between the "stoic resignation to necessity" of a
Marcus Aurelius and the "passionate happiness" exhib-
ited, for example, by "the Christian saints" (p. 41).

Yet James seems to have revived, momentarily, his old
enthusiasm for the strenuous mood in its unreligious reg-

ister when he wrote: "A life is manly, stoical, moral, or philosophical, we say, in proportion as it is less swayed by paltry personal considerations and more by objective ends that call for energy, even though that energy bring personal loss and pain." His next sentence is typical: "This is the good side of war, in so far as it calls for 'volunteers'": one almost expects him to write "heroes." "Such a man," he says, "is a high-hearted freeman," who "lives on his loftiest, largest plane" and "spurns the pinched and mumping sick-room attitude."

But, James now feels compelled to add, such a man does so by an "effort of volition," whereas the Christian saint does so by reason of "the excitement of a higher kind of emotion, in the presence of which no exertion of volition is required." That is why the former's "athletic attitude," even when most "stalwart," almost inevitably breaks down under the crushing weight of life's reversals—and comes to crave the consolations of religion. Urge "personal will and effort" on a person in this plight, and you will be suggesting the "most impossible of things" (pp. 45–46).

In the passages just quoted, James is chiefly preoccupied with contrasting the "moralistic" against the distinctively "religious" type of the strenuous mood. Traces of kinship remain, certainly, but he is deliberately stressing the "added dimension of emotion" which religious feeling comports, especially when one is facing down the evils of human life. His advocacy of religion's "enthusiastic temper of espousal" leads him to contrast it with the way "morality strictly so called can at best but bow its head and acquiesce."

But two observations are in order here: one, on his description of religion; the other, on his characterization of the "moralistic" attitude. In the first place, James is compelled to admit (p. 47n11) that there are people "in whose religious life this rapturousness is lacking": they are religious, but not in "this acutest sense" he wishes to describe "so as to get at [religion's] typical *differentia*." He has previously admitted (p. 42) that the gradations between ordinary and religious types of experience can be so continuous that it becomes difficult to draw any clear, firm line between them. To avoid the methodological difficulties in drawing that line, he has purposely chosen to describe "typical extremes," hence to consider religious experiences which are sufficiently "one-sided, exaggerated, and intense" as to differ unmistakably from non-religious experience.

My second observation is this: in that same zeal for contrast, James has (with the one momentary exception already noted) colored the moralistic attitude in tones that make it more difficult to recognize it as the "strenuous moral mood" of his earlier essays. Now, instead of the militant stride and knight-errant's jocund daring, he stresses the "frosty chill" of Marcus Aurelius' consent to his Logos (p. 42), the stoics's "drab discolored . . . resignation," the "dull submission" of the moralist who may "obey" the universal moral law but often "with the heaviest and coldest heart" so that he never feels it as anything other than a "yoke" (pp. 41–44).

More Positive Descriptions of the "Strenuous Mood"

But despite this somewhat negative characterization, James further on gives several descriptions of one type of saintliness (pp. 211–16) which seem to reinstate the more positive claims he had staked out for the natural strenuous mood in his earlier essays. One such description begins by portraying a certain kind of "character" which constitutes the natural base for any subsequent transformation by religious experience. The diversity of human types, he says, arises chiefly from our *differing susceptibilities of emotional excitement*," and the ways in which that emotional excitement can overcome our inhibitions. He proposes the example of a soldier faced with the dangers of battle: some "higher affection," when brought to a certain "pitch of intensity," can wield an "expulsive power" over the inhibitions which paralyze him from moving boldly into action, giving him the needed "pitch of courage" to accompany his comrades in their charge. Especially important to the "energetic" type of character he is describing is the "fighting temper," which manifests itself in subtler ways in "earnestness" of character: "Earnestness means willingness to live with energy, though energy bring pain." Now his reference point becomes explicit: "when the strenuous mood is on one, the aim is to break something, no matter whose or what." All obstacles, all psychic counterpulls are "trampled on with a ferocious pleasure the moment they offer themselves as checks to a cause by which our higher indignations are elicited." The counter-appeals of friendships, privileges, possessions suddenly count for nothing; "Rather do we take a stern joy in the stringency and desolation" brought on by renouncing them. "The great thing which the higher excitabilities gives," he adds in a note, "is *courage*." He then gives a list of "heroes" who had an "inborn genius" for such emotions: there would be many more of them were that inborn gift spread wider.

Now, *this* is unmistakably the "strenuous mood" of James's earlier essays. As though to remind us that he has been dealing with a pre-religious phenomenon, James proposes to "turn from these psychological generalities," in order to describe the analogous transformation worked by the "new ardor" which supervenes with religious conversion.

He returns to the same topic when setting the scene for his discussion of asceticism (pp. 239–41). Again, he begins on the natural, pre-religious level: we in the West "no longer think we are called on to face physical pain with equanimity," and yet "it is natural and even usual to human nature to court the arduous," for certain human types, at least. For them, "Passive happiness is slack and insipid," and they need a certain dosage of "austerity and wintry negativity, some roughness, danger, stringency and effort" to lend their existence "character and texture and power." Once the dosage is correct for the person

involved, he "is infallibly aware when he has struck it in
the right proportion *for him*. This, he feels, is my proper
vocation, this is the *optimum*, the law, the life for me
to live. . . . here I find the challenge, passion, fight and
hardship without which my soul's energy expires." Each
individual soul is different, of course; some "are happiest
in calm weather" only; but "some need the sense of ten-
sion, of strong volition, to make them feel alive and well,"
or else life's every accomplishment "comes too cheap
and has no zest" for them. These, James concludes, are
the types of natural character whom religious conversion
turns into ascetics.

James's final allusion to the strenuous mood (pp. 289–
94) occurs when he is endeavoring to overcome whatever
residual distaste his hearers might have for asceticism.
After all, he argues, asceticism "stands for nothing less
than for the essence of the twice-born philosophy" he
had earlier described: "the belief that there is an element
of real wrongness in the world, which is neither to be
ignored nor evaded," but "squarely met and overcome by
appeal to the soul's heroic resources, and neutralized and
cleansed away by suffering." For life, when all is said,
does seem to be a "tragic mystery," in the face of which
the "optimism" of the "once-born" type, who manages to
"close his eyes" to its "evils" and "sail through life hap-
pily on a healthy-minded basis," always seems a "shallow
dodge or mean evasion." So "mankind's common instinct
for reality" has always thought, and concluded that our
world is "essentially a theater for heroism." To this
"metaphysical mystery . . . recognized by common
sense," ascetics, despite their occasional excesses, have
always borne witness. Perhaps, James concludes, our
modern age, so much more given to softness and effemi-
nacy, could find in a revival of the ascetical ideal a formula for the "strenuous life," the "moral equivalent" we
desperately need for that barbaric school of heroism, war.

THE REALITY OF EVIL AND THE "TWICE-BORN"

Central to James's preference for the strenuous mood was
his conviction that human experience faced out on a uni-

verse where evils were real, deep-rooted, and genuinely dangerous. That conviction he articulates nowhere more insistently than in *Varieties*. So he describes religious happiness (pp. 47–49) as, not a "feeling of escape" from, but a "consent" to evils as exacting "sacrifice." Just as the figure of Satan, or the "negative tragic principle" in reality, adds to the "richness of the picture" Guido Reni painted of the archangel Michael, so the world itself is "all the richer for having a devil in it." Homer's unflinching recognition of life's evils makes his sense of the tragic more clear-eyed than the forced bravado of Whitman's "healthy-minded" optimism (pp. 77–78). In fact, this recognition that evils still remain to be overcome is James's criterion for deeming the "twice-born," the converted "sick-minded" person, as "formally superior" in type to his healthy-minded "once-born" counterpart (p. 138). True it is that individuals vary, so that the "god of battles" may be more appropriate to one, the "god of peace and heaven and home" for another. Granted, it may be extreme for the former type, the "twice-born," to look on the religion of their "healthy-minded" brethren as "mere morality." And yet, James stands to his guns:

> the outlook upon life of the twice-born—holding as it does more of the element of evil in the solution—is the wider and completer. The 'heroic' or 'solemn' way in which life comes to them is a 'higher synthesis' into which healthy-mindedness and morbidness both enter and combine. Evil is not evaded, but sublated in the higher religious cheer of these persons [pp. 384–85, 385n2].

PRAGMATISM AND THE STRENUOUS MOOD

The pages on religion written another five years later for *Pragmatism* (pp. 139–43)[11] breathe the same air as James's three latter treatments of the strenuous mood in *Varieties*: they conjure up, not the world of "wishing-caps" where "every desire is fulfilled instanter," but one that "grows under all sorts of resistances," one of "real adventure" and "risk." It requires a "normally constituted" individual with a "healthy-minded bouyancy" to accept its terms. Such a person knows he has "only a fighting chance," and must flail away manfully against "the bewildering accidents of so much finite experience," "*Top! und schlag auf schlag!*"

The world James's pluralism invites us to accept is one made for the "tough-" rather than for the "tender-minded," so much so that "Many persons would refuse to call the pluralistic scheme religious at all. They would call it moralistic," a world of "self-sufficingness," and reserve the term "religious" for the attitude of "self-surrender" appropriate to the world of monism. But, he replies, the monist's "religious optimism" may be "too idyllic" over the long run, "too saccharine." There must be *some* price to be paid in the work of the world's salvation, since the very "'seriousness' that we attribute to life" must mean that "there are genuine sacrifices somewhere, and that something permanently drastic and bitter always remains at the bottom of its cup."

James's option for a "moralistic and epic" kind of universe is rooted, as always, in his conviction that its evils are real and obdurate, that our "really dangerous and adventurous" world encloses "real losses and real losers." Hence anyone who would confront those evils with the requisite "seriousness" (read: in the strenuous mood) must be "willing to pay with his own person, if need be, for the realization of the ideals which he frames."

CONCLUSION: DEONTOLOGISM IN JAMES

The "strenuous mood," therefore—and all the stern deontological implications that went with it—occupied a central place in William James's ethical view, and not only for the James who wrote "The Will to Believe," but from beginning to end of his career. For our purposes here, that lifelong ingredience to his thought proves that there was nothing anomalous about its presence in his popular lectures. James's ethic was, to be sure, comprehensive enough to embrace eudaemonistic and teleological elements as well; but without his esteem for the battler, the hero, the martyr—without this "deontological streak"—James would be unrecognizable.

It was this deontological streak which saved James's "Will to Believe" from becoming a justification for wishful thinking; I have tried to respond here to the doubts which reviewers expressed about whether any such deontological streak existed. I hope I have presented sufficient evidence to show that James's high regard for the strenuous ethical mood clearly qualifies as a strong deontological component in his ethical thinking.

But James esteemed the capacity for, or, better, the preferential lean toward, living in the strenuous mood as so crucial a mark of human excellence that it served to guarantee far more than avoidance of the egoistic life lived in accord with "easy-going" ethical norms. Another service it rendered was that of preventing James's epistemological voluntarism from veering off into willful arbitrariness. To spell out that claim is still another task from the one shouldered here—another task and for another essay.

NOTES

1. See Patrick K. Dooley, in *Transactions of the Charles S. Peirce Society* 21 (1985) 569–76; Shannon McIntyre Jordan, in *Review of Metaphysics* 40 (1986) 137–38; John J. McDermott, in *International Philosophical Quarterly* 26 (1986) 189–91; and W. Tilley, in *Theological Studies* 46 (1985) 755. (I shall refer to these reviews by reviewer's name and page number).

2. (Montreal: McGill-Queens University Press, 1987).

3. See above, p. 121.

4. Dooley, *Pragmatism as Humanism: The Philosophy of William James* (Chicago:Nelson-Hall, 1974), p. 198n48. I would still strongly question whether MacLeod's article says anything unambiguous about the precise kind of precursive influence I claimed in my study, and would still hold that Edward Madden's remarks in this sense, in his Introduction to Volume VI of the Harvard University Press edition of James's *Works*

(1979), while recognizing the difficulties involved in this facet of James's position, fail to show how James deals with them. All citations of James's works are from this series (*The Works of William James,* ed. Frederick Bowers, 15 vols. in 18 [Cambridge: Harvard University Press, 1975–1988]).

5. Wernham refers to the sixth volume of *Works*, p. 161; he has chosen well, for pp. 159–61 contain James's distinction (from "The Moral Philosopher and the Moral Life") between the "strenuous" (sometimes called the "serious") and the "genial" or "easy-going" moral moods. Yet, as we shall have occasion to see, James has a good deal more to say on this distinction, some of which raises questions as to the argumentative use Wernham makes of this facet of James's thought.

6. See above, pp. 101–104.

7. Writers on ethics frequently distinguish "teleological" systems (in the sense in which I am here using the term "eudaemonist") from "deontologisms"—as though deontologism were *eo ipso* non-teleological. This seems to me a confusing classification: for in the subjective meaning of "teleological," one can "act purposively" by adopting as the purpose of one's ethical activity *either* the eudaemonist's aim of being "better off," *or* the deontologist's aim of "doing one's duty." The same is true of the objective, metaphysical meaning of the term: one can believe (or claim to know) that reality is structured "teleologically," i.e., so as to require and/or reward certain forms of subjectively purposive behavior, whether that behavior be of the eudaemonist or deontological sort.

8. See "Is Life Worth Living," in *Works* VI, p. 57.

9. I quote from the version of the "faith-ladder" contained in *Some Problems of Philosophy*, in *Works* VII (1979), p. 113.

10. *Varieties* dates from the years 1901–1902, "The Will to Believe" from 1896.

11. *Pragmatism* dates from 1906–1907.

Appendix B

Faith and Facts in James's "Will to Believe"

Several critics of my study of *William James on the Courage to Believe* were disturbed by what they saw as my voluntaristic interpretation of James's argument.[1] So strongly had I stressed the precursive force of the "will" to believe—not merely the "right" or "willingness" or "readiness" to believe—that I ran the risk of finishing, they opined, by leaving James's pragmatism entirely out of the picture.

Moreover, my critics might be thought to have excellent reason to accuse me of seriously exacerbating this voluntaristic view of Jamesian belief in a more recent article, where I tried to prove that there was a genuine "deontological streak" running through James's ethic. That deontological element, I argued, became crucially operative to keep the "will" to believe from becoming a wanton exercise in "wishful thinking."[2] But it could also be argued that the injection of a strong dose of deontology ran the risk of making the voluntarism I read into James's views that much more voluntaristic and, consequently, that much less pragmatically obedient to evidence—to "the facts."

Let me begin by conceding that there is a good deal of merit in such contentions, and, *prima facie* at least, good reason to be disturbed by such a voluntaristic posture. For James's more customary appeal to pragmatic verifi-

An earlier version of this essay appeared in *International Philosophical Quarterly*, 35, No. 3 (September 1991), 283–99.

cation has this much to be said for it: it is aimed at reining in our tendency toward "wishful thinking," toward believing as true whatever we want to be true—the "facts" to the contrary notwithstanding. It would *seem* self-evident that any conscientious thinker ought to take care to ensure that "the facts" warrant his believing that reality is as he believes it to be.

But it is important to notice that in the case before us we may be talking about "facts" of two distinct sorts, and it may be vital to keep those sorts carefully distinguished from each other. The first sort comprises the type of facts and interrelations of fact we take account of in elaborating our *Weltanschauungen*, our totalizing views of the universe. It is facts like these that we normally think of as deciding such issues as: whether life is worth living, whether we live in a universe that "makes sense" in moral terms, whether human actions are free or determined—and whether there exists a God Who stands as ultimate Guarantor of all the preceding. The reader familiar with James's famous lectures in popular philosophy will readily acknowledge that they testify to his burning interest in *weltanschaulich* questions like these—and that his focus in "The Will to Believe" is squarely on the last of those questions, concerning the theistic hypothesis.

But James also deals with another class of "facts" in these same lectures: let me call them (as I did in my study) "outcomes." Did the Alpinist succeed in vaulting over the chasm which confronted him? Or did the courageous young traveler successfully lead his fellow-passengers in an act of resistance which foiled the crooks who were resolved to rob them? In "outcome cases" like these, James thinks of the agent as possessing a robust "belief" that he can succeed in overcoming the challenge facing him. That belief he claims will be justified by a set of "future facts," represented by the successful outcome of his faith-inspired action. And if the belief is firm enough, James sometimes goes on to claim, it will "create the facts" of its own verification.

In my study of James's argument, I felt obliged first to

criticize James's rather wholesale claim that "faith creates the facts of its own verification."[3] I contended that
as a universal principle that claim would not stand up to
close analysis, and unnecessarily weakened the cogency
of his overall position. My criticism had the obvious effect of denying that those "faith-created facts" could
serve as evidential touchstones to verify pragmatically
the truth of the faith in question.

But my criticism went along with the additional claim
that James (and many of his loyal defenders) erred in
applying the "fact-creation" thesis, which they had mistakenly drawn from "outcome cases," to that quite different class of facts involved in instances of *weltanschaulich*
belief. This, I tried to show, was an entirely different kind
of faith from the one appropriate to outcome cases. Furthermore, I argued, James should have kept it clear in his
own mind and expressed it unambiguously in his prose
that this was the only kind of faith to which his "will to
believe" thesis could legitimately be meant to apply.[4]

But this *weltanschaulich* kind of faith, I then went on
to argue, was identical with the faith that James later describes as one that does not produce verification by "produc[ing] activity creative of the fact believed," but rather,
"without altering given facts," may be "a belief in an
altered meaning or value for them."[5] This shift in my argumentative focus would seem to have made my plight
even more perilous: having already eliminated the entire
range of "outcome facts," I have now swept the board
clean of the only other kind of facts which could conceivably serve as verification of our beliefs. This would seem
to leave James dangling in epistemological mid-air;
hence, the obligation I now feel to bring some clarity to
this troubling situation.

On Faith that "Creates the Facts" of Its Own Verification

First of all, I must make clear what I do *not* mean to
deny: if James's proposition about faith creating the facts

of its own verification were universally true, then those "facts" would satisfy the most conscientious pragmatist's demand for experiential verification, and (contrary to my argument) no voluntaristic pressure to produce a faith-assent would be appropriate. Now, James's illustrations of this claim are familiar to most readers: the Alpinist steels himself for a confident leap over a dangerous mountain chasm, or the railroad passenger acts out of the firm belief that bold action on his part will rouse his fellows to resist a band of robbers. In cases like these, James's contention would have it, the "vital heat" of strong belief will result in the success believed in. To the contrary, I objected, that confident faith *may* turn out to be *one* of several (or many) factors in the situation which *could* conceivably make for eventual success; but, I argued, this highly qualified truth falls well short of James's unvarnished guarantee that an ardent faith *will* in every case bring about that eventual success. That, I claimed, was going much too far.

But there is at least one serious objection to this contention of mine,[6] and it gains considerable plausibility from the way James's epistemology is usually understood; hence, it calls for careful examination. Recall for a moment my distinction between beliefs that lead to successful "outcomes," and beliefs—or what James *may* have meant by the term "over-beliefs"[7]—of a broader, *weltanschaulich* kind. A belief of the former kind, I conceded, *may* contribute to "creating the facts" believed in: the Alpinist's belief that he *can* do so may contribute to his leaping successfully across the mountain chasm. But, I queried, is the same thing true of a *weltanschaulich* belief like the theistic hypothesis? Can our faith truly "create the facts" that verify our belief that God exists? Or (to cite those other beliefs James focuses on in this same connection) can our faith "make it so" that life is worth living, that we live in a moral universe, that our actions are free and not totally determined? My answer was, no: to speak of our beliefs creating the facts which would make a *Weltanschauung* true or untrue simply does not make sense.

JAMES'S "M + x" ARGUMENT

But, to refute that negative verdict of mine, one need look no further, apparently, than James's own heady conclusion to the familiar "M + x" argument from "The Sentiment of Rationality" (*Works* VI, p. 84).[8] There it is unmistakably clear that James did take the view about our *weltanschaulich* faith that "'the world is good, we must say, since it is what we make it,'" and "'The belief creates its verification.'" But (to repeat my original contention) these quotations, which Professor Dooley's review has drawn from James himself, represent James's brave summary of the matter in its baldest, unqualified form.[9] And there is excellent reason for thinking that James came to change his mind in this regard.

Now, I cited these same quotations in my study,[10] expressly calling attention to the fact that they all come from pages 81–86 of that early essay. I refer to them as representing James's "provisional conclusion" from his M + x reasoning, argue that that conclusion will not stand up under careful analysis, and then lay stress on the fact that, in the *concluding pages of that same essay*, James clearly betrays his own awareness that this momentary seizure of optimism may have carried him too far. What I take to be the genuine conclusion to his essay (pp. 87–89) is couched in far more sober terms, and I, personally, am at a loss to find a single instance where James later goes back on that soberer conclusion.

To refresh the reader's mind on James's argument: "M" in his earlier equation represented "the entire world *minus* the reaction of the thinker upon it" and "x" the "thinker's reaction and its results." Then obviously "M + x"—standing for the "absolutely total matter of philosophic propositions" which will ultimately turn out as true of the world—will have a different value depending on how the "thinker" reacts and, by reacting, produces "results" which eventually contribute to the final composition (the "objective" M + x) of the world (p. 81). "M has its character indeterminate," James concludes some pages later, "susceptible of forming part of a thorough-going pessimism on the one hand, or of a meliorism . . . on the other. All depends on the personal contribution x." "The belief" that we meliorists have that we can make the world better "creates its verification" (p. 84).

How promptly, though, will that verification come? James presents what are actually two distinct versions of his answer to that question. The first of them comes immediately on the heels of his M + x argument, and assures us that the person who takes the world as moral and melioristic will, if the world be so in fact, "proceed to act upon [his] theory" and find it "reversed by nothing that later turns up as [his] action's fruit; it will harmonize so well with the entire drift of experience" that he will find himself in no way obliged to "change the essence of its formulation" (p. 86). His faith, in a word, will be pragmatically verified and, evidently, within the course of his life-experience.

If, on the other hand, the world be other than his theory hypothesizes, James assures us that the believer will "find himself evermore thwarted and perplexed and bemuddled by the facts of the world, and his tragic disappointment will, as experience accumulates, seem to drift farther and farther from that final atonement or reconciliation which certain partial tragedies often get"; in short, the theory will be pragmatically dis-verified by the accumulation of experienced facts which cohere more naturally with the counter-theory (p. 87).

Now, if this were James's last word on the question, the orthodox "pragmatic" interpretation would at least be accurately Jamesian: James's claim would be (rightly or wrongly) that a belief (like theism) will inevitably be verified (or falsified), confirmed, or "corrected" by subse-

quent experience. That subsequent experience, moreover, will be experience of a reality which has been
affected by the belief itself, "creating" the "facts of its
own verification." Hence, the argument goes, James turns
out to be definitely a pragmatist and not, as I was arguing,
a voluntarist. Nor have I the right to protest that the
crucial text has been drawn from a different lecture than
"The Will to Believe," since it is my own professed conviction that "The Sentiment of Rationality" is enough of
a companion to it that it may and must be allowed to cast
its interpretive light on "The Will to Believe."

But what I have called his "provisional conclusion" is
not, in fact, James's last word on the question. He has
written a second version of his conclusion which, as we
shall see presently, appears to have been composed some
time after the first. That second conclusion begins with an
admission which abruptly undermines the earlier version:
"for the sake of simplicity" he admits, he has "written
as if the verification might occur in the life of a single
philosopher." But that, he tells us now, "is manifestly
untrue." Why? Because over that short a span "the theories still face each other, and the facts of the world give
countenance to both." In a "question of this scope,"
James now admits, we should expect that "the experience
of the entire human race must make the verification, and
that all the evidence will not be 'in' till the final integra-
tion of things, when the last man has had his say and
contributed his share to the still unfinished x" (p. 87).

And so we are faced with what I labeled a "judgment-
day" type of verification which, I still hold, when it comes
to "the life of a single philosopher" in his capacity as
living believer, is, in strict rigor of terms, no verification
at all. But even if one wished to controvert that conclusion, this much is clear: in this "second" conclusion to
his essay, James has flatly denied his own earlier claim
that the "verification" of his faith could come to the individual believer within the span of his own lifetime.

HISTORY OF AN EMENDATION

I mentioned earlier that this "second conclusion" seems to have been written some time after the first one. My original reason for making that suggestion was doctrinal: the second conclusion so jars with the first as to seem, on the face of it, an afterthought consciously inserted to correct the provisional conclusion penned earlier.

But that doctrinal inference can be backed up by historical data, as well. We know that James wrote this essay in stages, revising repeatedly, deleting from and adding to the original matrix (see *Works* VI, pp. 326–27). The "M + x" reasoning had already appeared in his "*Quelques Considérations sur la méthode subjective*," written in 1877 and published in Charles Renouvier's journal *Critique Philosophique* (see *Works* I, pp. 23–31). The same argument features in his "Rationality, Activity and Faith" which he sent to the *Princeton Review* as early as 1879, though it was published there only in 1882. A letter to Charles Renouvier, written on May 8, 1882, complains about this delay in publication, but also goes on to mention that Renouvier had written about "an *abstention* on [James's] part to discuss certain cases of the formula M + x &c." James then adds that Renouvier "will observe that [James had] changed somewhat the ultra indeterministic conclusions of [his] old letter to your Journal": the communication, obviously, referred to above. His reason for those changes? "I thought I might have gone too far."

There is, obviously, matter here for informed historians of James's *oeuvre* to pursue; but these indications are enough to show that the M + x argument did represent a thorn in James's side, and that he came to wonder whether he had not "gone too far" in depicting the M in his equation as more "indeterminate" than was legitimate: and this was the central point in my criticism of that argument. There is, therefore, even stronger reason than I originally adduced for thinking that the "second conclusion" of "The Sentiment of Rationality" did, in fact represent a deliberate softening of James's earlier "provisional conclusion."

A FAITH WHICH DOES NOT ALTER THE FACTS?

James's emended version, however, contains an expression which could readily become a further bone of contention. James admits that, during the lifetime of any single philosopher, "verification" of a hypothesis like theism, for example, or of its opposite, is an impossibility. But the reason he gives for that stand-off is interesting: "the [competing] theories still face each other, and *the facts of the world give countenance to both*" (emphasis added).

In my original study, I linked phrases like this with others James uses to describe situations in which "the facts" themselves were incapable of grounding a decision one way or the other.[11] I coupled them with that distinction which James makes explicit in a letter to Horace Kallen, written in 1907, in which he describes a kind of faith which does not produce the facts of its own verification, but "may, without altering given facts, be a belief in an altered meaning or value for them."[12] Though written some eleven years after James's famous lecture on belief, that letter showed that James had, sometime before that date, come to explicit and reflective awareness of that distinction. But I also presented the evidence[13] showing that the distinction was already nibbling at the edges of his awareness in 1896, and that this semi-awareness partially accounted for the vein of pure gold that runs alongside the occasional dross marring certain passages in his earlier "popular lectures." To isolate the gold from the dross, I argued, the sympathetic critic should be willing to recast a number of passages from those earlier lectures and make them read as legitimizing the precursive intervention of the passional in the formation of our *weltanschaulich* "over-beliefs,"[14] and only those.

For these over-beliefs, I argued, were manifestly what

James had in mind as the instances of this second type of belief, which does not alter the "given" facts, the "facts of the world," but stage-lights them, so to speak, in such a way as to lend them a "meaning or value" different from those they suggest to the non-believer. So, for example, my coming to believe in God's existence does not *eo ipso* change any facts which were "given" antecedent to my act of believing; my act of faith does not of itself change the crime statistics, or make hurricanes less severe or cancers less painful: but (I take James to mean) without "altering" those given facts, my faith now enables me to view them in a certain light, from a certain perspective— to "draw a different conclusion from them," so to speak. My faith now enables me to "live with them," and presumably even act upon them differently from the way my non-believing brother does.

Moreover, this description of a faith that does not alter the given facts obviously does not mean to deny that "believers [in Dooley's terms] can and do" *go on* to "create" *a certain number* of "facts": "for example, when they show care and concern for their fellows thereby making the world [to *some* extent, at least] a better place . . ." (p. 572). Nor does my claim in any way imply that "choosing to believe or choosing not to believe in God changes absolutely nothing," since (the objector assumes) it condemns both believer and non-believer to be "paralytic spectators," unable to "'alter the facts in any way'" (p. 574).

THE STAGES OF BELIEF

An illustration may help to clarify matters. I suggest that James is thinking, in the first place, of a hypothetical person who is trying to make up his mind *whether to believe* that the world he lives in, say, "makes moral sense." He surveys that world, taking in as comprehensively as he can the "given facts," the "facts of the world" as they bear on the question at issue. Take the term "given" as (like the M of James's "M + x" equation) denoting the complexus of facts which that world presents, will he or nill he, for his inspection—as well as for the inspection of any comparable observer. Hypothesize for the moment that this survey is as neutral and objective as is humanly possible, since it antecedes the surveyor's taking any position, antecedes, in other words, any act of "faith" on his part which could "slant" or "weight" or "color" his view of the facts: they remain, in other words, as purely "given" as they can be, the "same" set of facts for the theist as for the atheist, for the determinist as for the libertarian, for the monist as for the pluralist. Now comes the question: what belief will our world-surveyor adopt? More pointedly, assuming that he did terminate his survey by posing some act of belief, what relationship will any act of belief he might pose bear to the "given facts"?

To this point, James's habitual answer is surprisingly negative: in *weltanschaulich* choices like these, "the facts practically have hardly anything to do" with what option the person will eventually make (DD 152), for "the opposing theories still face each other, and the facts of the world give countenance to both" (SR 107). This, I submit, is most plausibly what James meant by that crucial phrase in his definition of a "genuine option": the thought-predicament is perfectly illustrative of the kind of option *"which cannot by its nature be decided on intellectual grounds"* (WB 20; italics James's). If it were purely a question of which way the "given" facts point, James is saying (again!), the potential believer could never resolve his indecision one way or the other.

But, James is implying, when it comes to the kind of *weltanschaulich* faith we are *now* considering, it is never "purely" a question of which way the "given" facts point: they always point *for somebody.* And when the "given" facts are as irremediably ambiguous as we have supposed, the decision will, and must, depend on the decider, and on the decider's willingness to permit the "passional" to influence his decision starting from the very first move in his survey of the "facts."

For the hypothesis of a purely "neutral" observer of purely "given" facts "of the world" is, James insistently reminds us, exactly that: a hypothetical construct. But it is a useful construct, permitting us to trace the evolution of our faith options as though they occurred in distinct phases.[15] First, we have the "hypothetical" phase picturing a purely neutral observer of the "given" facts "of the world." If such an observer could exist, "the facts" would remain ineradicably ambiguous for him. In a "second" phase, we have what is always the actual reality: an observer voluntaristically "slanting" his survey of the "given" facts so that they become "the facts *for him*"— they now "point" toward the conclusion that the passional side of his nature deems acceptable. Now comes the third phase, perhaps only rationally distinct from the second, but with a distinction that puts order into our thinking: the observer decides for the option indicated by what have now become the "facts for him." Finally, in a fourth phase, the observer, now become a believer, "acts out" his faith by "creating" a set of "world-altering" facts (call them "consequent" on his belief, like the "x" of the M + x equation) in line with what he has come to believe.

We shall see presently that James gives a number of examples which illustrate the faith-stages just described as proper to phases two and three. But my contention for the present is this: both these stages represent a faith which has "altered" the "meaning and value" which the antecedently "given" facts of the world have for the believer, *without actually altering those facts themselves*, and without as yet issuing into the (phase four) "faith-consequent" activities whereby the believer sets about altering the world. Now, it should be obvious that this description in no way denies that, once he has made his decision *for* belief, the believer may, even should, strive to "alter the facts" of our world *on the basis of* that belief. But the "facts" we are *now* talking about are no longer what James intends by the "given facts" of our world, and the fact-altering activity in question, along with the facts "created" by that activity, are *consequent* to belief.

Verification by "Consequent" Facts

But an orthodox Jamesian would have every right to raise now a question which is far more relevant to James's pragmatism: can the array of "consequent facts" serve as pragmatic verification of the believer's faith? No one would seriously doubt that "believers can and do create facts" when "they show care and concern for their fellows, thereby making the world [of *consequent* facts] a better place." What I am questioning is whether Professor Dooley is entitled immediately to append the claim (p. 572) that this "better place" of consequent "facts . . . would verify belief in God." And it remains my conviction that that claim is neither objectively sound nor authentically Jamesian.

As to the claims's objective soundness, it seems fairly evident that while believers can (and, indeed, should) strive to alter the facts of our world, they are normally able to alter them only within certain limits. Choosing to believe in God and act on that belief may not go so far as to empower the believer to change everything he or she would long to change; and making the world a *somewhat better* place may not make it *so good* a place as to "verify belief in God" beyond all residual ambiguity. And we shall shortly see that James was lucidly aware of that residual ambiguity.

Clearly, then, both James and I were arguing for the legitimacy of belief; we were both commending belief on the shared assumption that our faith should influence our activity, and so result in *some* real changes, however modest, in the world about us. This was precisely the root of my difference with James L. Muyskens's contention that James would be better understood as justifying, not belief, but "hope": the hope Muyskens advocates did not seem to me the efficacious font of action that James's "strenuous mood" seems to require.[16] But while it is Jamesian to insist that faith issue into consonant activity, it is far from "Jamesian" to believe that *each* of our individual faiths, issuing into whatever beneficent actions they may engender, can *so* change the face of the universe we live in, *so* alter the evidential situation confronting other potential believers, that the total ensemble of "facts" of that ameliorated universe will argue peremptorily for theism over atheism.

Where the Difference Lies

But obviously, one major pivot of my interpretation of James's lecture is the view I have espoused of James's famous "M + x" argument from "The Sentiment of Rationality," complete with its corollary that the second, emended version of that argument will not sustain the twin conclusions that this world is simply "what we make of it," and "The belief [that it is good] creates its own verification" (Dooley, p. 575).[17] But it should also be clear that my claim entails the refusal to treat "over-beliefs" and "outcome beliefs" along the same lines, and notably, an insistence on a uniformly factual basis for pragmatically verifying *all* our beliefs, including those which are *weltanschaulich* in nature. Perhaps the most satisfying way of resolving any remaining doubts on these issues is to find out whether the first, or the the second, "soberer," version of James's M + x argument is endorsed in his later works. Does the later James, in other words, require (as several of my critics would contend) pragmatic verification of our *weltanschaulich* beliefs? We shall have to confront that issue shortly.

"The Will to Believe" in James's Later Works

Before advancing to that question, however, I should clear the decks of another possible position: perhaps, it might be argued, I have not dealt with Professor Dooley's position at its full strength. He may not be thinking of the changes that can be wrought by an individual believer, but speculating, rather, on the possibility that as more and more humans act—by the thousands, the millions—in Jamesian style, the world may thereby be changed more and more for the better. In that case, "the facts" of *that* improved world might no longer be so ambiguous as to "give countenance to both" the opposing theories James is dealing with. Granted, that might be simply a speculative flight, but it could be illuminating to see whether there is any textual support for considering it as in any sense Jamesian.

That question brings up still another: several of my critics queried whether my entire interpretation of the relatively early "Will to Believe" would stand up to examination in the light of James's subsequent development.[18] Two features of my interpretation call for particular attention: first, what happens, in James's later writings, to the sweeping claim he made in the "provisional" conclusion to his "Sentiment of Rationality" that "faith creates the facts" of its own verification? And, second, does he confirm or weaken my claim that his "will to believe" thesis legitimately applies only to *weltanschaulich* faiths, and that such faiths may confer a new meaning upon, but without themselves altering, the "given" facts of reality?

Does Faith Create the Facts of Its Own Verification?

I have not, in the first place, been able to find any identifiable trace of the "fact-creation" claim in *The Varieties of Religious Experience* (1902). But in *Pragmatism*, written some four or five years later, James is arguing (pp. 136–37; 142–43) for his melioristic way of understanding the proposition that the "world can be saved." For the pragmatistic thinker, he explains, the question comes down to whether or not the world's salvation is a "concretely grounded" or "well-grounded" possibility. But what does that expression mean?

First, James replies, "there are no preventive conditions present, but . . . some of the conditions of production of the possible thing actually are here." For a chicken to be "concretely possible," then, there must be no "self-contradiction" in the idea of "chicken," no "boys, skunks, or other enemies about," and at least one "actual egg" in existence. "As the actual conditions [including 'actual egg—plus actual sitting hen, or incubator, or what not'] approach completeness the chicken becomes a better and better-grounded possibility. When the conditions are entirely complete, [actual chicken] ceases to be a possibility, and turns into an actual fact." Always, of course (the reader feels compelled to add), provided that any armies of boys or hordes of skunks can be kept out of the act!

Now, says James, apply this analysis to the (clearly *weltanschaulich*) question whether the "salvation of the world" is a concrete possibility. "Pragmatically" this would mean that

> some of the conditions of the world's deliverance do actually exist. The more of them there are existent, and the fewer preventing conditions you can find, the better-grounded is salvation's possibility, the more *probable* does the fact of the deliverance become.

This, James goes on to argue, is how his attitude of "meliorism" views the matter: it sees the world's salvation as neither impossible nor inevitable, but "treats it as a possibility, which becomes more and more of a probability the more numerous the actual conditions of salvation become" and, one is tempted once more to interject, the more whatever "preventing conditions" which may exist are overcome. For any such "ideals" to become realities, they must first be "grounded" in "live champions" such as we ourselves are; then, "if the complementary conditions come and add themselves, our ideals will become actual things." What does he mean by those "complementary conditions"? "They are, first, such a mixture of things as will in the fulness of time give us a chance, a gap that we can spring into"; let us call that the "objective" side of the matter. From the subjective side comes the complement of that: "*our act.*"

Now James comes to the question that concerns us here: "Does our act *create* the world's salvation . . . not the whole world's salvation of course, but just so much of this as itself covers of the world's extent?" Boldly he asks, "*Why not?*" That bold queston comes down to mean, why should we not take our actions at what seems to be their face-value, as the "turning-places and growing-places . . . of the world," the only places and ways the world may grow: *pace* the monist whose block-universe theory insists that, rationally, the only agent of the world's growth must be "the integral world itself." But, James admits, his pluralist theory implies that "the wishes of the individual" he has supposed as crucial in the world's growth "are only one condition." There are other individuals, indeed "all sorts of resistances," in his pluralistic world, so that the world "grows . . . from compromise to compromise, only gets organized gradually" (if, in fact, his reader whispers the hope, it gets finally organized at all).

Ponder this complex, carefully hedged, and at bottom very guarded claim, where our individual wishes (and beliefs, presumably) are "only one condition" among many, and compare it with the relatively simplistic optimism of the uncorrected "M + x" reasoning of "The Sentiment of Rationality," and it is plain that James has come a considerable distance.

In *A Pluralistic Universe*, written a year later, James ends his final lecture by explaining the "faith-ladder" which (as we shall see further on) is the route which, he claims, all thinkers follow in deciding between those two major *weltanschaulich* options, pluralism or monism. His hearers will undoubtedly make their personal options, he observes, on equally non-logical grounds. "And [their] acting" in accordance with the option they have made "may in certain special cases be a means of making it securely true in the end" (p. 148). Faith, expressed in actions, *may,* and *in certain cases must,* be *a means:*

surely the steam has gone out of his earlier unqualified conclusion!

Some Problems of Philosophy, on which James was working the very year he died (1910), touches on the same issue in an "Appendix" entitled (significantly) "Faith and the Right to Believe" (pp. 111–13). Here he presents a series of contrasts between what he terms the "intellectualist" and the "pragmatist" views of the world. Summing up the latter, he proclaims his evolutionary belief that "work is still doing in the world-process, and that in that work we are called to bear our share." But "our share" is, manifestly, only part of the story.

Hence (I italicize the relevant terms) the provisional tenor of his conclusion: "The character of the world's results," he says, "*may in part* depend upon our acts. Our acts *may* depend on our religion,—on our not-resisting our faith-tendencies, or on our sustaining them in spite of 'evidence' being incomplete." These faith-tendencies, he goes on to say, are "expressions of our good-will towards certain forms of result" and are for that very reason "extremely active psychological forces, constantly out-stripping evidence" (pp. 112–13). "Extremely active" they may be, but we are given no specifics on the *extent* of their efficacy to "create" the "forms of result" they aim toward. The explicit admission, furthermore, that our faith tendencies are "constantly out-stripping evidence" could explain why they may require "sustaining" against the doubts that could spring from that absence of verification. But while that may come down only to restating the truism that faith always remains faith, it also effectively discards as authentically Jamesian the contention that our faiths can be counted on to create the facts which remove all such "doubts," so that our faith-tendencies need no longer be "constantly outstripping the evidence."

There follows, somewhat abruptly, a description of the "faith-ladder" which the believer mounts stepwise from thinking a certain *Weltanschauung* might, then may, ought, must, and finally "*shall* be true, at any rate for *me.*" No "intellectual chain of inferences," James admits, this ladder of "faith" is the expression, rather, of our "good will, our 'will to believe'" that we live in a pluralistic universe "requiring the good-will and active faith, theoretical and practical, of all concerned to make it 'come true.'" "Requiring," yes: but *guaranteeing* that it will come true? Again, James's statement is far more measured than it once was.

His conclusion is equally measured: he ends by warning his "intellectualist" adversary that rejecting the legitimacy of such a believing attitude would "debar us from ever admitting that [pluralistic, melioristic] universe to be true." Is that quite the same, though, as assuring us, in positive terms, that adopting the will to believe will issue into verification that such a universe is "true"?

In sum, my contention on this particular issue closely resembles Smith's: [19] James had every right to claim that "belief in the *possibility* of the outcome's having a certain character is, or may be, a factor producing the result." For in cases where "antecedent belief in the possibility of success [in leaping over a chasm, for example] affects my effort in a positive way, then I have contributed *in some measure* to the outcome if it is successful." Hence "the belief is 'true' about some aspects at least of the total situation in which it figured." But that guarded claim corresponds far more closely to what James wrote in his later works, and only remotely to the provisional conclusion of his earlier "M + x" equation.

The Two Kinds of Faith in James's Later Works

Finally, I submit that James's later works confirm his acceptance of the kind of faith which I described as proper to phases two and three in the foregoing analysis. A faith of this sort, James tells us, "may, without altering given facts, be a belief in an altered meaning or value for them."

Perhaps the classic, and classically paradoxical, formulation of this kind of faith occurs, precisely in reference to the theistic hypothesis, in *The Varieties of Religious Experience.* On pages 202–206 James presents a number of quotations to illustrate that feature of the religious conversion experience which he describes as "the *objective* change the world often *appears* to undergo" (emphasis added). This is how he refers to that paradoxical experience when the objective world *itself* seems to have been endowed with a "clean and beautiful newness" which the convert had not detected there before. And yet James makes it evident throughout that the convert is nevertheless beholding the very same "objective" world of "given facts" as he did before, and as his non-converted fellow humans still behold.

Returning to the same paradox on page 373, he explains how prayer can "temper" us into becoming more *receptive* to the world as it religiously *is:*

> The outward face of nature need not alter, but the expressions of meaning in it alter. It was dead and is alive again. It is like the difference between looking on a person without love, or upon the same person with love. . . . We meet a new world when we meet the old world in the spirit which . . . prayer infuses.

The parallelism with his description to Kallen of the "second kind" of faith is striking, but less surprising in that both texts are roughly contemporaneous.

But James remains substantially consistent in the years that follow: in *Pragmatism* (pp. 9–12), though less dramatically than in his descriptions of religious conversion, the same effect is attributed to the root "philosophy" which "determines the perspective" each of us brings to our several worlds. James makes it clear that he is not using "philosophy" in its technical meaning, but is referring to that "dumb sense," rather, of what life deeply means, "our individual way of just seeing and feeling the total push and pressure of the cosmos." That (call it a pre-reflective) "posture," that personal way of seeing, not this or that particular but everything within our ken, that "temperamental vision," gives each of us "a stronger

bias" than any objective premises. It "loads the evidence
. . . one way or the other," in favor of tough- or tender-
mindedness, and therefore, as succeeding lectures make
clear, in favor of any one *weltanschaulich* option over its
opposite member: in James's own case, for empiricism
over rationalism, pluralism over monism, freedom over
determinism, pragmatic meliorism over absolute forms of
either optimism or pessimism, and so on.

Further on, James's language becomes distinctly value-
laden: the opposing visions are traced to "healthy-" *vs.*
"sick-" or "morbid-mindedness." Indeed, we all have our
"moments of discouragement," and as humans can be
"healthy minds one day and sick souls the next," and
so, in consequence, "see" the same objective world in
different terms. But, he continues, as philosophers we
must frankly and consistently adopt one form of vision
over the other, knowing full well that, in the end, "it is
our faith and not our logic that decides such questions"
(pp. 139–42). Once again it is clear from the context that
both "healthy" and "morbid" minds are looking out at
the very same universe. The "given facts" are the same
for both of them; it is their "faith," their "temperamental
vision," which decides how they "see" that identical
world of facts in the most universal terms. But, in addition, James seems to suggest that being philosophical requires that one freely choose consistently to adopt one
perspective over its competitor; and, one assumes, he
means by this that we both should and can adopt the
"healthy" rather than the "morbid" way of viewing
things.

A Pluralistic Universe, from 1908, stresses that same
precursive quality, but this time James speaks of all philosophers as having their personal "visions, modes of
feeling the whole push, seeing the whole drift of life": he
is implying, again, that our *Weltanschauungen* rise up
from the passional part of us. But here he describes those
visions as "forced on one"—not by the facts or by theoretical considerations, but—"by one's total character and
experience, and on the whole *preferred*—there is no

other truthful word—as one's best working attitude."
Those visions, however, clearly correspond to mind-sets
(or heart-sets) which James thinks are in place *before*
the person takes on the conceptualizing and generalizing
efforts (which are beyond the "primitive" mind's capacity) involved in technical philosophizing.

But does this conceptualizing effort work toward tem-
pering, or correcting, the pre-technical vision? James's
answer to that question may be unsettling, but it comes
to this: once the generalizing intellect awoke, "then began
those divergences of conception which all later experience seems rather to have deepened than to have effaced,
because objective nature has contributed to both sides
impartially, and has let the thinkers emphasize different
parts of her, and pile up opposite imaginary supplements"
(pp. 14–15). In this dense and somewhat tumbling sentence, I submit that "divergences of conception" clearly
refers to the competing philosophic systems which have
emerged from the competing pre-philosophic "visions"
he has been speaking about. One might have hoped that
"later experience"—a presumably common experience
of "objective nature"—might gradually have "effaced"
those "divergences" of conception; but it has instead, in
James's view (alas?), only "deepened" them. For instead
of contributing a steady stream of unambiguous evidence
for one side and against the other, "objective nature has
contributed to both sides impartially, and has let the
thinkers emphasize different parts of her"—in accord, obviously, with the priorities implicit in their initial, pre-
technical "vision." Clearly, though, James here remains
thoroughly consistent with his earlier view, that diametri-
cally opposed though their *Weltanschauungen* may be,
their proponents nonetheless behold the very same "objective nature," the identically same world of "facts."

His closing remarks (pp. 147–48) return to the same
point: he has just explained that pluralism and monism,
as he conceives of them, "make pragmatically different
ethical appeals"; but he must confess that, despite all his
preceding theoretical arguments, his hearers will decide

between those competing world-views "just as [their] own sense of rationality moves and inclines" them. For "One's general vision of the probable is what usually decides such alternatives." And at this point James makes a casual admission as unembarrassed as it is explicit: the mechanism he has just described corresponds to what he once "wrote of as the 'will to believe.'"

He then goes on to illustrate how such decisions are made; he sketches, once again, but now more fully than before, what he calls his "faith-ladder": it moves from first entertaining a certain non-contradictory "conception of the world," then thinking that it "*might*" be true, then that it "*may*," then that it "is *fit* to be true." That fittingness passes into "it would be *well if it were true*, it *ought* to be true" until it becomes a "*must* be true." The ultimate conclusion is a highly personal "decision": "It shall be *held for true*, you decide; it *shall be* as if true, for *you*." "Not one step in this process is logical," James insists, "yet it is the way in which pluralists and monists alike espouse and hold fast to their visions." But the implication, again, is that both pluralists and monists behold the same factual world. Hence what James goes on to say can fit either party: this faith-decision "is life *exceeding* logic, it is the practical reason for which the theoretic reason finds arguments *after the conclusion is once there*" (italics mine).

CONCLUSION: FAITH AND FACTS

To sum up: when asked whether a belief is validated by the evidence of "facts," James replies by bringing two sorts of facts into play. When striving to illustrate his thesis about "willing" to believe, he first proposes an array of "outcome" cases, and argues from them that faith can "create the facts" which then serve as its verification: if the Alpinist, for example, believes firmly enough that he can do it, he will succeed in vaulting the abyss which yawns at his feet.

I have tried to show that there are at least two features about such outcome cases which preclude their answering to the needs of James's argument: first, that even in outcome cases, faith cannot be counted on to ensure success in every instance; as even James came later to recognize, there are too many other factors whose efficacy needs to be taken into account. But, second, the argument from outcome cases is irrelevant to the issue at hand, for his popular lectures, including "The Will to Believe," attest to the fact that James is really concerned with another kind of faith: he is concerned with our faith in *weltanschaulich* issues like the existence of God. And this, in turn, implies that he is interested in another kind of "facts." Although he attempts, in one instance and (so far as I have been able to find) one instance only (in the "M + x" argument), to equate such issues with outcome issues, obviously hoping thereby to bring faith in *weltanschaulich* issues within reach of his pragmatic method of verification, careful attention to the chronology of his writings shows that he came to realize the vanity of that attempt: no individual philosopher can hope to verify a truly *weltanschaulich* belief within his own lifetime; his faith stubbornly remains exactly that, a faith.

Is there no possibility, then, of justifying our faith in *weltanschaulich* propositions by consulting "the facts"? Having already answered that question in the negative, James confirms his negative answer by calling attention to the crucial difference between the kind of faith which can produce activity which "alters" the facts, and another kind of faith which does not alter the facts, but lends them an altered meaning or value. A moment of reflection, along with James's own later observations, again shows that he views this latter as the kind of faith we repose in *weltanschaulich* propositions, like the existence of God. But, James contends, it is equally evident that "the facts themselves" are the same for both believer and unbeliever; hence, neither party can appeal to those facts for "verification" of one belief over its contradictory.

This is why James repeatedly insists, both early and

late, that our "passional nature," our "will" to believe in one side of the argument over the other, must be allowed to settle the issue. But our inveterate sense of epistemological responsibility still protests: is this no more than a reversion to something like "wishful thinking"? Granted that what decides such questions may not be evidence swaying the intellect, but grounds which move the will, there must still be some criterion for distinguishing when those grounds are legitimate and illegitimate. Does James furnish such a criterion? No defense of his celebrated lecture can claim to be adequate unless it answers that question satisfactorily. I hope to furnish a loyal attempt at an answer to that question in Appendix C.

Coda: A World Without Evil?

One final remark about a possibility raised by James's idea of a melioristic universe. Above, I briefly alluded to the possibility that if sufficiently large numbers of human beings acted energetically on their theistic-*cum*-melioristic belief, the world could conceivably be made so much better a place that "the facts" would eventually attest unambiguously to the rightness of that belief. I have searched for a text which would show James encouraging that notion, in vain.

There are, however, a number of texts which prompt the conviction that James would have rejected that possibility. Edward Madden refers to several of them while dealing with the nettling question of evil and its quasi-necessary place in the Jamesian universe (*Works* VI, pp. xv; xxv–xxvi; xxxii): it almost seems that James is convinced that "there *ought* to be evil . . . to make heroic action necessary" (*Works* VI, p. xxxii). Human freedom, James maintains, would have no pragmatic value if the "world were nothing but a lubberland of happiness already" (*Works* [Pr], p. 61).

James makes the same point with his *fictio* of the Creator proposing to mankind the style of universe they would legitimately prefer: his own choice falls, predictably, on a universe in which mankind would constantly have to collaborate with His activity by braving and overcoming evils (*Works* [Pr], pp. 136–39). Madden sums up well, if a trifle broadly: "it was inconceivable to James that anyone would resist the call to do battle in a good fight" (*Works* VI, p. xxvi); moreover, he seems to have felt unquestioningly that this was the permanent condition into which mankind would always be born.

His reaction to the experience of a stay at the Chautauqua Assembly is emblematic: in time he came to feel it was the very paragon of the "lubberland" of happiness, the "foretaste of what human society might be, were it all in the light, with no suffering and no dark corners." "This human drama without a villain or a pang," James sums it up, "this atrocious harmlessness of all things—I cannot abide with them." He would prefer to take his chances again "in the big outside worldly wilderness with all its sins and sufferings," for he aches for that element of "precipitousness . . . of strength and strenuousness, intensity and dangers" which makes the human world the arena of "everlasting battle," and yet, for that very reason, the only cradle of (that vintage Jamesian word) "heroism" (*Works* X, pp. 152–53). These, James was convinced, were the essential ingredients which would forever define the human scene. Assuredly, changes, improvements can and should be made in certain aspects of that scene, but we must not "expect that they will make *any genuine vital difference* [italics James's] on a large scale to the lives of our descendants. . . . The solid meaning of life is always the same eternal thing," and "those philosophers are right who contend that the world is a standing thing, with no progress, no real history. The changing conditions of history touch only the surface of the show" (*Works* X, 166–67).[20]

These counsels have, at first reading, a surprisingly pessimistic ring; one is tempted to discard them as thoroughly un-Jamesian. But they only bring to its logical expression one of the man's central convictions: to be truly significant and rewarding, our lives must be open to the call of heroism, to the demands of the strenuous moral mood. This, he was convinced, was something that our moral universe would always require; belief in that moral universe would, accordingly, never be a question of yielding to the preponderance of evidence, even the evidence we might produce by acting loyally, and perhaps heroically, on our belief. There would always be moments when we would be challenged to leap courageously beyond the ambiguities of the evidence, and lend that evidence meaning and value through our resolute *will* to believe.

NOTES

1. See, for instance, Patrick Dooley's review in *Transactions of the C. S. Peirce Society*, 21 (1985), 569–76. But a similar complaint is implicit in John J. McDermott's suggestion, in *International Philosophical Quarterly*, 26 (1986), 189–91, that there was a good deal more pragmatism in his lecture than I had given James credit for. Page references to both reviews appear in parentheses in my text.

2. "'The Will to Believe' and James's 'Deontological Streak'" in *Transactions of the C. S. Peirce Society*, 28 (1992), 809–31, substantially reproduced above as Appendix A.

3. See above, pp. 70–83.

4. Ibid.

5. See ibid., p. 71. Dooley, 576n10, objects that a "close look" at the letter to Kallen discloses that "James *did not* distinguish between some beliefs which produce their verification and others which do not" but that "beliefs produce verification in two distinguishable ways, and that in some cases, verification may occur after the believer is dead." Dooley seems to be reading the letter to Kallen through the lens furnished him by the *uncorrected* version of James's unfortunate "M + x" argument (which we shall examine shortly). This is tantamount to claiming that this kind of *post mortem* verification can count as "pragmatic" verification for the living believer himself, since only this latter kind of "verification" can be at issue.

6. I pass over Dooley's contention (p. 570) that I should

have taken to heart what John Smith writes on p. 39 of his *Purpose and Thought: The Meaning of Pragmatism* (New Haven: Yale University Press, 1978). There Smith warns against alleging that "'James confused the logical consequences of a proposition or hypothesis with the consequences of *believing* the proposition or hypothesis.'" Dooley's thrust goes doubly wide: first, because his quotation from Smith fails to sum up my objection at all accurately, and, second, Smith is not speaking here about "The Will to Believe" at all, but about faulty criticisms aimed at James's paper of 1898, "Philosophical Conceptions and Practical Results." In note 84 to the very next page of the volume in question, however, Smith does make a point à propos of "The Will to Believe": he speaks of the possible "confusion between the consequences (implications) of a doctrine, and the consequences of believing that doctrine." But, Smith goes on to admit, he does "not claim that there is nowhere in James" any instance of such a confusion! This is much more relevant to the criticism I was making in my analysis; but more on that analysis shortly.

7. Implied here is an interpretation of what James seemed to intend by the expression "over-belief" (i.e., an over-arching *weltanschaulich* belief). There are a number of loci where, implicitly or explicitly, James intends the term this way (*Pragmatism*, pp. 9–12; *A Pluralistic Universe*, pp. 14–15, 148; *Varieties of Religious Experience*, p. 405). But he seems to have veered (later on?) to using the term differently: it comes to mean a general proposition (though less universal than "belief" in the *weltanschaulich* sense of "The Will to Believe") whereby we use "reason" to "build out" interconnections from passional beliefs of the "Will to Believe" sort, to construct a scaffolding of generalities both dependent on, and supported by, them (*Varieties of Religious Experience*, pp. 165, 402–405). The citations for these and for all of James's works are taken the series *The Works of William James*, ed. Frederick Burckhardt (Cambridge: Harvard University Press, 1975–1988).

8. The following abbreviations are used for the "popular lectures" cited from that volume: WB for "The Will to Believe"; SR for "The Sentiment of Rationality"; and DD for "The Dilemma of Determinism."

9. Dooley's argumentative tactic here is puzzling, for in quoting that same passage in his book on *Pragmatism as Humanism* (Chicago: Nelson-Hall, 1974), p. 87, he enters several

important qualifications: "the actions this belief promotes actually *help* to produce a melioristic universe," he writes, and our faith "*helps* to create," is "*one of the factors bringing about* verification" of our belief. These are saving qualifications indeed, and perfectly in line with my criticisms of James; but they raise the question why Dooley contents himself, in his review, with the flat declaration that "The belief creates its verification."

10. See above, pp. 77–80.

11. See above, pp. 81–82.

12. See above, p. 71.

13. See agove, pp. 70–71, 88–89.

14. See note 7, above. For Dooley's dismissive account of this hypothesis on James's growth in reflective awareness, see his review, p. 571.

15. Indeed, James's "M" in his "M + x" formula corresponds almost exactly to the "given facts," neutrally observed, which I hypothesize here.

16. See above, pp. 75–76.

17. Dooley here makes a series of pronouncements with which (given his misunderstanding of my position) he seems to fancy I would disagree: that "over-beliefs have an enormously real (and practical) impact upon our actions and the future of the world," and that "moral or immoral actions of flesh and blood human beings [settle] the world's fate." (To which I reply, "No problem"). From belief in God, he continues, "all sorts of actions naturally and spontaneously flow." (I could not agree more).

18. John J. McDermott posed this same query in his review. Notice, however, that there is a slight anomaly imbedded in this demand: if clear traces of his "early" doctrine can be found in his later works, James's basic consistency may be considered to create a certain presumption in favor of my interpretation of those earlier works; but if not, I can always claim that the later James simply changed his mind—as indeed I claim he quite demonstrably did about the validity of his famous "M + x" argument.

19. *Purpose*, p. 61.

20. Quotations are from "What Makes a Life Significant," which James first delivered in 1898, the visit to Chautauqua having occurred in summer of 1895. See *Works* XII (1983), pp. 237–43.

Appendix C

James's Voluntarism: Readiness, Willingness, or Will to Believe?

In the two foregoing studies, I have endeavored to show that in his famous lecture on "The Will to Believe," William James was arguing that we humans came to the formation of our *weltanschaulich* beliefs in a way that has this surprising feature: our passional nature exercises a precursive influence upon both the experiential process of data-gathering and the intellectual process of understanding and evaluating those data. The notion of conducting a coolly objective because utterly dispassionate survey of the evidence *before* allowing our "willing" side to exercise any influence on the conclusions we drew from that survey was, James argued, a myth. Not only was this precursive intervention of the passional a psychological fact (to which the conscientious philosopher of knowledge may feel obliged to reply with a disheartened "alas!"), but James argued that this was the way our process of belief-formation *legitimately* worked.

When I published my *William James on the Courage to Believe*, I fully expected to hear a strident chorus of "Nays" greeting that precise point. But, to my surprise, only one reviewer protested; even then, his protest took a peculiar form. For he found no difficulty whatever in admitting that "our passional demands tremendously influence both our beliefs and over-beliefs"; indeed, he wondered why I thought that was "news" at all! And yet an instant later he seems to have sensed that my view of "precursive influence" was not quite the one he was comfortable with: "tremendous influence" he warns, "is not preemptory influence." For "James, the voluntarist is also James, the pragmatist" who reminded us that believers, engaged in action as they must be, "are unavoidably presented with experiential evidence which corrects or corroborates their passionately induced beliefs."[1] It would appear, then, that having depicted precursive influence as "preemptory" in force, I have made James out to be so bald a "voluntarist" that he is no longer recognizable as an authentic pragmatist. For the honest pragmatist will always look to experiential evidence to eventually "correct" any passionately induced beliefs which could, presumably, turn out to have a faulty fit with the facts.

There is no question that Dooley has touched here on a neuralgic point. From the perspective of a responsible epistemology, James's position as I have described it would seem *prima facie* illegitimate: my analysis appears, at least, to make James out to be an unbridled voluntarist, and not to make sufficient allowance for the way his pragmatism should presumably work to tame that voluntarism with the corrective curb of "experiential evidence."

Yet Dooley is honest enough to admit that our passional side "tremendously" influences the formation of our "over-beliefs," like theism. Indeed, on five different occasions in his book on the humanism of James's thought, he goes so far as to characterize that influence with the term "control," a control which issued from the "structures of human nature" itself; and nowhere does he hint that those structures are amenable to modification.[2] So Dooley, too, might well have seen the need for facing the difficulty squarely: in the terms he himself uses, how can we truly expect "experiential evidence" to "correct" a "passionately induced" belief, when the same passional inducements still remain in "control" of our cognitive powers as they go about the business of doing the correcting? "Tremendous influence is not preemptory influence," Dooley decrees—a ringing affirmation, certainly. Furthermore, in his review, that compromising term "control" has been carefully muted. But does this new set of expressions really direct our understanding toward a way out of the dilemma? I think not.

MADDEN'S VERSION OF THE PROBLEM

But the problem is not peculiar to Dooley; Edward H. Madden, too, on page vi of his introduction to Volume VI of James's *Works*, which contains "The Will to Believe,"[3] candidly admits that the influence of the passional side of our nature is precursive, for "James never retracts his blunt statement that the intellect is *subordinate* to the affections" and "the willing aspect of life . . . dominates both the conceiving and the feeling [i.e., sensory] aspects." Shortly afterward, however, Madden hastens to assure his readers (p. xviii) that in James's brand of "voluntarism and fideism" terms like "subordinate" and "dominate" must not be taken to mean that "affective and volitional elements determine decisions beyond the capacity of the individual to control" but "rather that affective and volitional elements have a legitimate epistemic rôle to play in reaching certain decisions."

But if the volitional does not "determine" the belief-decision, does not "control" the individual's assent, what, precisely, is its "epistemic rôle"? Madden admits (p. xix) that James's "strongest statement of his volitional view" seems to occur in the essay "Reflex Action and Theism" (1881) where James writes that the willing aspect of the self "dominates" the conceiving and perceiving aspects. Some pages later Madden sums up James's view as holding that "personal and volitional elements are never wholly absent from anyone's thought" and that "in some cases they play a decisive role, legitimately leading equally honest people in different directions" (p. xxxviii).

Now, I suggest that these statements, taken as an ensemble, leave the reader less than satisfactorily enlightened. Closer consideration of what Madden has written may further sharpen the problems nesting in James's voluntaristic fideism. Surely, as Madden points out, James

himself must bear some of the onus for creating this confusion—in this connection Madden's story (pp. xv–xx)
of James's repeated "vacillations" back and forth from a
"strong sense," a genuine "will" to believe, to the weaker
sense of a "right" to believe is worth pondering.

But just as surely some measure of the confusion is
Madden's as well. How exactly is one to characterize a
volitional influence that "dominates," "subordinates,"
acts "decisively" upon our knowing powers, but stops
short of "determining" their operation? The quandary
only deepens when we observe that, having underlined
the importance of that essay, Madden has nonetheless
refrained from quoting from it what is certainly *the*
"strongest expression"—and, I submit, the clearest—that
James gives of his position. In "Reflex Action and Theism," speaking of the "demands" that the will has "the
power to impose" on our cognitive activities, James affirms that "Our volitional nature must then, until the end
of time, exert a constant pressure upon the other departments of the mind to induce them to function to theistic
conclusions" (WB 101). Not only *does* the will have this
power of "imposing" its "demands," it "must" do so, in
order to guarantee that we become and remain theists.

What Is in Our "Control"

That statement of James's position, however, compels us
to reconsider Madden's assurance that, for James, the
"affective and volitional elements" of our nature do not
"determine decisions beyond the power of the individual
to control." (Otherwise, Madden argues, James would
have been advocating either skepticism or some variation
of the "sociology of knowledge," conclusions which Madden assumes we will view as unacceptable.)

There is, however, a small puzzle tucked away in using
expressions like "control," as both Madden and Dooley
have done. Let me illustrate it this way: assume, for the
sake of argument, one of the more usual views of our

cognitive activities, and you will think of our minds and senses as, ideally, so utterly receptive as to be "determined" by the "evidence"—incapable of seeing black as white, or two plus two as adding up to anything else than four. These are rudimentary cases, however. Now take a question quite different in scale: is the "individual" (to use Madden's term) who is faced with the cosmic panorama of evidence *pro* and *con* the existence of God equally "determined" one way or the other?

The usual view would seem to imply, assuming we may divide the individual's "mind" into James's three "compartments" (WB 91–93), that the conceiving mind and the senses *should* remain perfectly "objective"—i.e., they should permit themseves to be determined by each item of evidence in turn, then by how those items relate to each other; then, the decision on how the assemblage of evidence "adds up" should be equally determined by the pattern which the "objective evidence" has, of itself, assumed. Meanwhile, the will should stand aside, not interfere, should allow all these determinations to produce their natural effect on the mind and the sensorium.

But if that be the case, the final decision of the "individual" will be as determined as the operations of mind and senses are. In short, the decision, in Madden's terms, turns out to be "beyond the power of the individual to control." But suppose, as James does, that the individual's mind and senses are under the control of his will, then (James himself would expostulate) what could be more *in* the "power of the individual to control" than his own free will?

To this one might object that the "will" may be one factor in the situation, but what (for example) of the subject's affectivity? One might argue that affective leanings, especially if long-standing and deeply rooted, may impede the freedom of, or otherwise unduly limit, the will's activity, and so place the individual's "decision"—on the theistic hypothesis, say—"beyond" his control. Unless, unless. . . . Assume, as James's language frequently implies, that theism is the sane and healthy hypothesis every normally constituted individual *should* ideally embrace,[4] then it seems plausible to infer (what James seems to have inferred) that it should be in the power of the moral agent to will such a crucially moral act. Hence (the inference is as old as Aristotle), the individual by his or her free will should be able to gain such control over affectivity as to "induce" it to collaborate in commanding the cognitive powers to render their judgment in favor of that hypothesis.[5]

Now, James is obviously convinced that such free-will control of our cognitive powers is not only possible, but in certain instances actually appropriate and desirable. Furthermore, in such cases, and only in such cases, would the "decision" in favor of theism be "in," not "beyond," the "control of the individual" making it. And only in such cases could one qualify such a decision as "ethically good" or "bad," "healthy" or "sick"—the decision a moral human being "ought" to make, or the reverse.

"Will" vs. "Willingness"

This topic of control brings up another issue which has frequently been raised in this connection, one dealt with in my essay in a way that several of my reviewers seriously misconstrued. One can speak of the will's exercising over the cognitive powers a kind of control which is "weaker" or "stronger," or of a strength (or various intensities of strength) intermediate between the two. One could, accordingly, envisage these differing "strengths" of will-pressure as issuing, *grosso modo*, in a mere "readiness" to believe, or in a more positive "willingness" or in a resolute "will" to believe. Or, working from a slightly different point of view, one could claim (as James did more than once) that his essay was unhappily titled, since he was arguing only for the "weaker claim" that in cases like the theistic hypothesis we have a "right" to believe. On that reading of the matter, James would not be arguing for the "stronger claim": that there are circumstances when we have something approaching a "duty," and *ought* to exercise a positive "will" to believe.

JAMES'S METAPHORS OF BELIEF

Now, the perspective I assumed for handling these distinctions was that of examining the various "metaphors" James employs in arguing for the legitimacy of belief.[6] Those metaphors wove their way in and out of his argument, but they were, I claimed, of different sorts and as such, they presented differing kinds of justification for belief.

Consider two of them now, in the order of their respective "strength," as that term was used just above. First, James alludes several times (WB 22 and 28) to how a measure of belief must enter the process of making friends: we must "believe" that the other's expressions of interest and dawning fondness are sincere and truthful if we are ever to make friends with him or her.

James's next two metaphors may be telescoped into one, for the metaphor of the Alpinist's belief that he can leap across a mountain chasm resembles that of the brave individual steeling himself (and, he hopes, his fellow-passengers) to rise and thwart a band of train-robbers: both these illustrations aim to stress the point that in such risky ventures a robust belief in the prospects of succeeding will ensure—or at least contribute to ensuring—a successful outcome.

Now compare these illustrations. Observe how "strongly" James supposes our "strong" belief will exert its influence in the Alpinist or train-robbery cases. Both predicaments are fraught with danger, fear, and uncertainty; both demand a faith compounded with boldness, manliness, fighting spirit. In both these illustrations, one feels little or no compunction in talking about a "will" and perhaps even a "duty" to believe, especially if a robust manly belief could (as James thought) truly be counted on to "create the facts" of its own verification.

The belief appropriate to "making friends," however, is of a markedly different sort, and James gives every indication of acknowledging that difference. Instead of a belief whose very strength might "extort" friendship from the other, he speaks of "trust and expectation," of "meeting the other half-way," of showing a "trusting spirit." There is all the difference in the world between this tentative, hesitant, tactful kind of faith and the Alpinist's muscular belief which would aspire to "create the facts" of its own verification. Surely, when speaking of making friends, one may talk of a "readiness," a "willingness," to believe. But a "will" to believe? Hardly.

In my essay, I had several times called the reader's attention to Gail Kennedy's article in which he tried to show that James should be interpreted as arguing for just that modest a claim: we are entitled to a "readiness" or "willingness" but not to so strong an attitude as a "will" to believe.[7] At this point in my treatment of James's several metaphors, I reminded the reader "once again" of Kennedy's thesis by saying: "All this [discussion of the friendship metaphor and its implications] would appear to argue, once again, that James was largely correct in eventually repudiating the 'will' to believe, and might have been better advised to speak consistently of a 'willingness' or 'readiness' to believe from the very outset."[8] And, indeed, *if* the metaphor of "making friends" were the only one guiding James's pen, Kennedy's contention *would be* sound. But my prose was shaped to warn the reasonably careful reader that my conclusion was entirely hypothetical: moreover, the entire context alerts that reader that there *are* other metaphors for belief in play, and that James may have thought that *their* force entitled him to make the stronger claim: for a "duty" and a corresponding "will" to believe.

Strangely, both Dooley (p. 571) and McDermott[9] refer to the above conclusion, and speak as though they took it as both categorical and final, when it is clearly neither.[10]

McDermott sees that my remarks concerning a "willingness" to believe bear on this friendship metaphor, but he may not have noticed that their bearing is *limited* to that metaphor. The force of the "Alpinist" and "robber-band" metaphors, I still claim, is robust enough to justify (during the crisis moments of our faith-lives) a genuine "will" to believe. Hence, the title of my study: James, at his most alert, was arguing for the "courage" to believe, or to continue believing, when life's challenges make it hard to do so.

Notice, however, a distinction to which I failed to do justice in my essay: that this same metaphor may acquire stronger force when it is question of "keeping" a friendship. Here, one might readily envisage circumstances where something like a "duty" and a consequent "will to believe" could come into play, i.e., where one ought, out of loyalty, to believe in a friend's truthfulness, say, or innocence, even though the weight of evidence appears *prima facie* to be against him.[11]

Let me say it once more: I acknowledge that James was not always perfectly lucid, nor always consistent in making his case, and that he came on several occasions to say that he *should* have confined himself to maintaining the weaker claim that we had a "right" to believe.[12] In spite of that, however, I would still argue that his earlier essays, when read in a generous spirit and sifted for the philosophic best they have to offer, provide cogent grounds for this contention: there are certain circumstances when we not only may but *ought* to sustain the "pressure" (or "control") of our will (or "passional nature") upon our cognitive powers, so that those powers will collaborate in coming to one sort of *weltanschaulich* conclusion rather than its opposite. For responding to the appeal of a life lived in the "strenuous" moral mood can sometimes require no less than that. And the strenuous mood, James is convinced, is so evidently superior to its "genial-mood" competitor that we both may and should prefer it as a reliable clue to the moral character of our universe.

The "Will" to Believe in James's Later Works

So much for my claim about his earlier lectures: what, though, of James's subsequent works? Does he, even while dealing more focally with the "substance" of belief, remain consistent with what he has earlier prescribed about the correct attitudinal "approach" to belief?[13] The question has several facets, all of them interconnected: does James, in the first instance, soften the "pressure" (which, I have claimed) he once described our passional side as precursively exerting, and even prescribed that it ought to exert, on our intellectual processes? Is he, secondly, consistent in characterizing the source of that influence as "will" or, more generally, the "passional" side of our nature? And, finally, is he consistent in the way he accounts for our "preference" or "choice" of one style of world-view against its competitor—and does that account square with the interpretation I have advanced?

Madden correctly points out that the strongest expression of James's voluntaristic emphasis occurs in the quite early essay on "Reflex Action and Theism" (p. xix), that James never retracted that "blunt statement" of his view (p. xi), but defended "the same core of claims" over a span of some fifteen years (1881–1896), thus showing the "continuity and importance of these themes in [his] thought and life" (p. xix). But, he adds, there is a "development from the earlier to the later pieces," a softening of his initial voluntarism, that is, in the years from 1881 to 1896. Hence, one might suspect, as Madden and others have also suggested, that there may have been a further development in the works written after 1896. Though not directly a question of interpreting the earlier essays, it could indirectly confirm my interpretation of them if James's later thought can be shown to run along lines consistent with it.

James's description of "conversion" in *The Varieties of Religious Experience* (*Works*, pp. 170–74) might initially appear to belie any such consistency; there he distinguishes between the "volitional" and the "self-surrender" types of religious conversion, and goes on to say that he does not see the difference between them as "radical," since "Even in the most voluntarily built-up sort of regeneration there are passages of partial self-surrender interposed." Furthermore, in most cases "when the will has done its uttermost towards bringing one close" to the complete "unification" conversion betokens, it seems that the "very last step" must be one of "self-surrender" to those "other forces" beyond the person's inner resources, whose existence and activity are *felt* in religious experience: the personal will must actually be "given up" in this terminal phase of "yielding."

Before the process reaches its culmination in self-surrender, however, it would be idle to assure the man painfully conscious of his sinfulness that "all is well" with him; that would sound cold-bloodedly false to him; he cannot be expected to consent to such assurances, for "'The will to believe' cannot be stretched as far as that." Notice that that incriminating expression does not seem to frighten James overmuch.

James later stresses this sense of higher forces at work in the conversion process (*Works*, p. 197) and the correlated need for "acquiescence" rather than positive volition (*Works*, p. 201). This would all seem to downplay that energetic streak of voluntarism which justified his speaking earlier of a genuine "will to believe." And yet, as we shall have occasion to see in another connection, that is not his last word on the subject, even in *Varieties*.

Pragmatism, however, intimates a different message. Its opening remarks quote Chesterton to the effect that the "most important thing about a man" is his overall "view of the universe," or, using the term in an informal sense, his "philosophy." For it "determines" his entire "perspective" on the universe—a vigorous characterization of its influence, surely, but perhaps with just that trace of rhetorical hyperbole that should warn us to be cautious. In any case, though, it soon becomes clear that James is talking about what he had earlier called a person's "faith."

But what accounts for one man's having one, while another has another such "view"? James replies with the term "temperament"; this is what gives even the "professional philosopher" a "stronger bias than any of his more strictly objective premises," making him, *in specie*, an empiricist rather than a rationalist, a pluralist rather than a monist, "tough-" rather than "tender-minded"—or, of course, the reverse of all these (*Works*, pp. 9–13). That key term, temperament, he never defines, nor does he accord it any technical study worth talking about anywhere in his *Principles of Psychology*. But he cannot have been so innocent of such matters that he failed to realize he was encouraging his readers to trace the root of their personal philosophy to a stratum of the personality which is generally conceived to be inborn, permanent, and scarcely amenable to later alteration. Hence, the scary inference that our temperament "determines" our worldview, which in turn "determines" our perspective on all particular matters in that personal world. This would be strong stuff, indeed.

When he returns to that topic in his final lecture, however, that difference in "temperament" is expressed in more evaluative terms: now it separates "sick-" or "morbid-minded" souls from the "healthy-minded." These two tendencies are also at war within each one of us; and yet "There is a healthy-minded bouyancy in most of us," and if we are "normally constituted," that bouyancy will point us toward choosing to view the universe as a "moralistic and epic kind of universe" from which "the element of 'seriousness' is not to be expelled." Here the "strenuous" moral mood is obviously uppermost in his mind, and it leads him to speak as though the "adoption" of the melioristic view of the universe over its competitors were a question of our choosing, our "willingness" to respond to our "author's" urging.

We must all choose, James goes on to say, between the securities of monism and this risky universe of pluralism, and we can make that choice in either a "healthy-" or a "sick-minded" way. Indeed, "as human beings we can be

healthy minds on one day and sick souls on the next."
But "as philosophers," i.e., serious philosophers "aiming
at clearness and consistency, and feeling the pragmatistic
need for squaring truth with truth," we must choose
cleanly between the two. We must, in other words, settle
for either the "tender" monism or the more "robustious"
healthy-minded pluralism for which James himself, quite
obviously, has opted. But while our commitment to
"clearness and consistency" may compel us to choose
one side cleanly enough to preclude all compromise with
its antithesis, James abstains from saying that that commitment, of itself, dictates *which* of the two sides we
should choose. On what grounds, then, is that choice to
be made?

James answers with a rhetorical question: "Doesn't the
very 'seriousness' that we attribute to life mean that in-
eluctable noes and losses form a part of it, that there are
genuine sacrifices somewhere, and that something permanently drastic and bitter always remains at the bottom
of its cup?" The language, clearly, is again that of the
"strenuous" moral mood; James is implying that while all
of us may attribute "seriousness" to life, we may not all
choose to "see" our universe in the moralistic, even tragic
terms which alone are consistent with that attribution of
seriousness.

How, then, is such a choice made? "In the end," James
replies, "it is our faith and not our logic that decides such
questions, and I deny the right of any pretended logic to
veto my own faith." That faith he goes on explicitly to
characterize as one which views the universe as calling
forth the "strenuous" moral mood: a universe which is
"really dangerous and adventurous," in which there can
be "real losses and real losers," an "epic" kind of universe in which one must be "willing to pay with his own
person, if need be, for the realization of the ideal which
he frames" (*Works*, 141–43). This is still the James we
know from his earlier lectures: not logic, but a passional
kind of faith guides our fundamental philosophical decision—faith in a moral universe, which exacts of us a life

lived in the strenuous moral mood. But now a fresh
question arises: is it merely "temperament" that decides
our primal option for us, or a "choice" we ourselves make
between moral "sick-mindedness" or "healthy-mindedness?" This, and not so much the attenuation of his voluntarism, may well be the true direction in which James's
thought is developing.

A Pluralistic Universe (Works, pp. 14–15) again speaks
of one's personal "vision" of the world as the great fact
about anyone, but again, the context shows that the term
"vision" comes down to meaning the same thing as the
"faith" James spoke of in Pragmatism. But that vision, he
now tells us, is the "expression of a man's most intimate
character," and "all definitions of the universe are but
the deliberately adopted reactions of human characters
upon" the universe. This is why reading a typical history
of philosophy is somewhat like paging through
an album of photographs: we find ourselves passing
"from one idiosyncratic personal atmosphere into another." Those various visions, though, really come down
to a few types, "just so many visions, modes of feeling
the whole push, and seeing the whole drift of life, forced
on one by one's total character and experience, and on
the whole preferred—there is no other truthful word—as
one's best working attitude. Cynical characters take one
general attitude, sympathetic characters another." Thus,
the cynic's thinking normally tends toward materialism,
while the "sympathetic" mind prefers a spiritualistic
view, and so on down the line. "Intimate character," "deliberately adopted reactions," "preferred" attitudes—to
account for our primal faith, James is reaching more and
more boldly for the language of responsible moral choice.

Toward the end of that same work (Works, p. 148),
James expresses his hope that the theoretical considerations proposed in his lectures have at least established in
his hearers' minds that pluralism is a "fully coordinate
hypothesis with monism" (which, living in the Oxford atmosphere, he knows they are likely to favor over pluralism). But theoretical considerations are one thing: his

hearers will, he admits, undoubtedly choose one or other rival view as their "own sense of rationality moves and inclines" them. For, once again, "one's general vision of the probable usually decides such alternatives. They illustrate what I once wrote of as the 'will to believe.'"

Here, surely, we have witness to that consistency in depth which Perry found marking James's thought from start to finish. But we are also being told how the later James construed his own earlier thought on the "will to believe" which lies at the root of our various primal philosophies. Never once has he suggested that our preference derives from the objective evidence to which we are severally exposed; it arises, on the contrary, from the way in which that evidence is reacted upon by "our own sense of rationality," our own "general vision of the probable," the shape and thrust of our individual "will to believe."

At this point, James presents the "non-logical" sorites to which he refers as his "faith-ladder," and presents it for all the world as though it was the way he envisaged now the mechanism of that earlier "will to believe." "No step in this process is logical," he insists, "yet it is the way in which monists and pluralists alike espouse and hold fast to their visions. It is life exceeding logic, it is practical reason for which the theoretic reason finds arguments after the conclusion is once there."

What can we conclude from all this? And, first, did James, in his later works, soften the rigorous influence on our cognitive powers which his earlier essays seemed to attribute to the "passional" side of our nature? We have seen that in *Varieties of Religious Experience* James subordinates the "volitional" factor in religious conversion to a more passive "surrender" to the "higher powers"; they, it would appear, eventually bring the convert around to accepting the fresh view of the universe which he then embraces. Indeed, if *Varieties* were all we had to go by, we would have to conclude that James considered the "will" to believe, before that moment of "surrender," as strictly limited: it could not "stretch" so far as to bring the unconverted subject to embrace the religious view of things. Linked with this motif is a kind of passivity in the whole conversion process which would suggest that one speak less of a "will," and more of a "readiness" or "will-ingness," to believe.

Pragmatism concerns itself, however, with the more "philosophical" aspects of our *Weltanschauung* forma-tion; in one of his strongest expressions for its influence, James roundly says that our root philosophical attitude "determines" our several "perspectives" on the world. That language suggests as strong an influence as ever he held for in his earlier lectures, but at the same time a certain softening may be entering from another quarter: having first attributed our adoption of one such world-view over another to our "temperament," thus re-opening the possibility that our world-views are imposed on us in quasi-deterministic fashion, he makes a series of remarks further on which bid us to be cautious in drawing any such inference. For the somewhat neutral term "tempera-ment" is replaced by the more value-laden terms "sick" and "healthy," and James would have us observe that all of us have known swings from "sick-" to "healthy-mindedness" and back again. Indeed, he goes on to imply that we have the power to control those mood-swings.

Perry, we know, once argued that "it is impossible to avoid the inference that a proper spiritual hygiene would bring a man to that better spiritual state in which plural-ism is palatable—that the strong man eager for battle and enjoying the risk"—the man who can respond to the chal-lenge of life lived in James's "strenuous mood"—"is the more ideal type." Levinson, for his part, disagrees: Perry, he claims, has underplayed the continuity between James's "moralistic" views (which Perry prefers as the "real" James) and his religious thought. James the student of saintliness was led to conclude that "in many ideal characters, the line between health and sickness blurred, and a sense of quiet assurance complemented the strenu-ous life." Besides, adds Levinson, "James never firmly stood behind these diagnoses of pluralism and monism" (as healthy- and sick-minded, respectively), "much less drew the inference" Perry would have us draw.[14]

Despite Levinson's demurral, however, I am strongly inclined to view James's religious thinking as presenting a slightly atypical picture when compared with the somewhat later, more philosophical, and "moralistic" *Pragmatism*. To bolster Perry's suggestion it should be added that *Pragmatism* once again directly links our choice of the pluralistic "faith" with our preference for a life lived in the "strenuous" moral mood, and it forges that link precisely in the final chapter, entitled "Pragmatism and Religion." That same work clearly intimates that we can "choose" to make that strenuous mood our "preferred working attitude." It remains a possibility of Jamesian thinking, therefore, even if he never actually brought it to expression, that humans can reflect on their own swings from sick- to healthy-mindedness, then consider the appeal of a world demanding a life in the strenuous moral mood, and freely decide to embrace that kind of world despite what their initial "temperament" might formerly have led them to prefer.

It is not always easy to decide how far one may interpret James in full rigor of the terms he employs, but his remarks in *A Pluralistic Universe* almost seem calculated to encourage the conclusion that what formerly was merely a possibility of his thought has here come to overt expression. The "faith" he spoke of earlier has now become a personal "vision" of the universe: no great alteration there, of course. But now, even while speaking of personal "idiosyncrasy," he roots that personal vision, not in our temperament, merely, but in our "most intimate character," and goes on to speak of "all definitions of the universe" as "but the deliberately adopted reactions of human character upon it." Our individual visions are "forced on" us, but "by [our] total character and experience." Evidently thinking of those mood-swings from morbid- to healthy-mindedness of which he spoke in *Pragmatism*, he now leaves room for a "*preferred*" way of seeing things, and preferred because we have come to acknowledge it as "our best working attitude."

If James is saying what he means, and really means what he says, he is here placing our commanding vision of the universe far more "in our power" than some of his earlier formulations would have led us to suspect. James does not explicitly refer to the fact that we are each born with a certain temperament, and have no choice in the matter; but the shift from inborn temperament to "total character and experience" cannot have occurred entirely unawares. He has now placed it squarely in our power to reflect upon our own mood swings, and "deliberately adopt" one of our moods as consciously "preferred" over its opposite. The resulting "vision" still commands, we may presume—perhaps (in the expression James used earlier) it still "determines"—how we take account of particular facts in the objective world, but now we have been placed, far more explicitly than formerly, "in command" of choosing that personal vision.

On what grounds do we prefer, deliberately adopt one primal vision of the universe over its competitor—in this instance, the "pluralistic" over the "monistic" view of reality? It is not "objective nature" which accounts for that choice. Inspect the opposing philosophies history presents us with, and you will find that "objective nature has contributed to both sides impartially," and all "later experience seems rather to have deepened than to have effaced" the "divergences" springing from those competing initial visions (*Works*, p. 15). Though he is brought to mention it but once (*Works*, p. 57), and then only in passing, there is every reason to believe that James still considered it preferable to opt for a world where human life is lived in the "strenuous mood." For he remains convinced that "philosophy is more a matter of passionate vision than of logic . . . logic only finding reasons for the vision afterwards" (*Works*, p. 81), and James's own "passionate vision" of the world as pluralistic was always bound up with his belief in that world as risky, adventurous, hence calling forth the full resources of our bravery, even heroism.

James's later works support, therefore, the conclusion indicated, more tentatively perhaps, in his earlier popular lectures: though he is initially tempted to credit our "temperaments"—an innate endowment over which none of us can hope to exercise control—he eventually comes round to situate the radical determinant of our individual "faiths," our affectively charged world-views, in our fully formed "character." And James is clear on this: we do have a significant measure of responsible control over the formation of our character.[15]

In fact, in James's eyes, our most crucial achievement as free and morally responsible human beings is the building of a character which will become the reliable agency of morally good actions. And everything we have seen suggests that he would hold as primary among those "good actions" the adoption of a *Weltanschauung* which is congruent with good moral activity—the kind of activity, we can safely conjecture, which issues from the "strenuous moral mood." But, to James's mind, what ultimately makes the strenuous mood superior to its easygoing counterpart is its correspondence to the kind of "moral universe" which, he is profoundly convinced, we inhabit. One of his favorite and oft-repeated maxims assures us that persons of the strenuous mood are more closely attuned to the heart-beat of Nature itself: *vim naturae magis sentiunt.*[16] James felt that his choice of a moral philosophy, and of a corresponding epistemology, was corollary to his choice of an ontology: the ontology of a moral universe.

What accounts, then, for our choosing rightly when it comes to embracing the most fundamental set of options life solicits every human being to make? Those options, James replies, all have to do with whether we are in profound sympathy with our universe as moral; those options are, in consequence, uniformly moral in nature. It follows, then, that the human equipment adapted for making the choice correctly must be equally moral in nature.

To choose rightly in matters as over-arching as these, one must be a person of developed moral character. And while it may not be in our "control" to be intellectually brilliant, it is in our control to become a person of character. So, it is only right that a moral universe should lay down as its conditions for recognizing its true nature, that one choose what that universe places within reach for each of us to choose, if only we will it.

But we must now confront the question which must rightly disturb the conscientious epistemologist: where does the process of pragmatic verification come into all this? To make it slightly more manageable, frame the question this way: once a person has adopted one *weltanschaulich* "vision" over its competitor, does James ever allow for any real possibility that subsequent experience will "verify"—or falsify—the truth of that vision? Since theism is at the heart of James's "will" to believe discussion, allow me to limit the question even further: does James give us any grounds for thinking that experience will ever provide evidential verification—or counter-verification—for our "belief" that God exists? If so, we have a right to call him a pragmatist; if not, we may have to admit that he is, at bottom, a voluntarist. Which will it be?

One locus which immediately comes to mind is the famous "M + x" argument from "The Sentiment of Rationality." But we have seen that its promise of verification is deceptive, and that James appears to have corrected his initial conclusion to show that he came to realize as much.[17] Another locus that comes to mind is James's adjuration in "Reflex Action and Theism" that our willing compartment should exert constant "pressure" on our cognitive faculties to assure that they come to theistic conclusions:[18] this, clearly, is much more an expression of voluntarism than of pragmatism.

In fact, practically everything we have seen thus far would argue that in the final analysis James's voluntarism wins out over his pragmatism. *Pragmatism* might at first seem to contradict that conclusion, for there (*Works,*

p. 99) he aims a "Woe" at "him whose beliefs play fast
and loose with the order which realities follow in his experience: they will lead him nowhere or else make false
connections." But inspection of the context shows that
James meant by "realities" here only such particulars as
"things of common sense . . . or else common-sense relations, such as dates, places, distances, kinds, activities."
This has nothing to do with verifying the kind of over-
arching view such as theism represents. And our problem, remember, concerns the epistemological conditions
for verifying precisely the kind of *weltanschaulich* vision
James was concerned with in his popular lectures.

The fact is that each time James confronts the precise
issue of verifying the theistic hypothesis, he winds up
admitting that it is, in the last resort, beyond verification
in any meaningful sense. He had appealed, in the "second
conclusion" of "The Sentiment of Rationality," to what
I have called a "judgment-day" verification; but he was
compelled to admit that any such verification could never
occur within the lifetime of any individual philosopher—
it was not, therefore, a verification which, for us the living, could have any meaning here, now, tomorrow, or
forty years from now.

Never, since that early essay, has James been faced
squarely with this question of verifying theistic belief and
come forth with a statement in any way rivaling the con-
fidence of that earlier view—a view by which, singular
and isolated though it is, Dooley sets such store.

But, Dooley argues (p. 572), "believers can and do create the facts (for example when they show care and concern for their fellows thereby making the world a better
place) which would verify belief in God." Apart from his
equating "outcome" and what I have called "over-belief"
situations, Dooley seems to make belief in God (for the
Jamesian) tantamount to believing in a "melioristic" universe. Now, I never meant to question that James insists
that genuine belief will flower forth into the kind of practical activity which makes the world a "better place." But
I question once again whether this proof that the world's

"M," in James's terms, is indeterminate *enough* that the "x" of our actions which make it *in some measure* a "better place" truly amounts to "verifying" that our world is "melioristic" in the full sense that James attributes to that term. But, secondly, I fail to see how the world's capacity to be made a "better place" can be taken as "verifying" that God does, indeed, exist. What is more to the point, however, I cannot find James himself making that claim anywhere except in the over-hasty "provisional conclusion" to the "M + x" argument which, we have seen, he later chose to express in more chastened terms. Aside from that provisional conclusion, however, I strongly question whether a later instance can be found in James's writings where he asserts that, precisely in respect of a *weltanschaulich* hypothesis like theism, "believers are unavoidably presented with experiential evidence which *corrects or corroborates* their passionally induced beliefs" (Dooley 575; emphasis added). Search James's works and each time he directly addresses himself to the "pragmatism and religion" issue, he sedulously abstains from making any such "verification" or "falsification" claim.

Follow the argument in *Varieties of Religious Experience* and James seems to be aching to find grounds for just such a claim. He expatiates on the "convincingness" of religious experiences to the one *experiencing* them (*Works*, pp. 66–67), on the "facts" of "mind-cure" which assure *its adherents* that the world is wider than science normally admits (*Works*, pp. 102–105); the relatively passive character of the conversion experience persuades *the convert* that "higher powers" exist and act upon us (*Works*, pp. 185–86). But then (*Works*, pp. 263–64) he comes to the crucial question: can we measure the worth of religion's human fruits "without considering whether the God exists who is supposed to inspire them?" Obviously not, but to settle such questions we would have to be "theologians," and James (precisely *qua* pragmatist?) is clearly unprepared to make that claim for himself quite yet!

The evidence shows the saint to be a noble human type, he says further on (*Works*, pp. 297–300), yet the key question in judging whether the saint or the Nietzschean strong man represents the higher human ideal turns on whether the unseen world the saint believes in truly exists. Then, in a pair of admissions which are quite remarkable coming from a pragmatist, he says: "It is [religion's] *truth*, not its utility," which, his hearers will rightly insist, should govern our verdict; "It goes back" once again "to the question of the truth of theology." In hopes of answering that question, James asks us to turn to the witness of the mystics.

James leads us through a lengthy survey of the testimony of and about the mystics; remarkable human types, again, their mystical experiences also resulted in impressive effects on their lives; *they* were firmly convinced that the unseen world existed. But once again, instead of settling the question, all of this only compels him to return to the necessity of evaluating the "truth" of their claim (*Works*, p. 329). But can philosophy come to some reliable settlement of this (quite unpragmatically framed) question of "truth"? James's conclusion on that question comes on page 359: "In all sad sincerity I think we must conclude that to demonstrate by purely intellectual processes the truth of the deliverances of direct religious experience is absolutely hopeless."

Continuing with his examination of religious phenomena, James probes into those "other characteristics," chief among them prayer; prayer seems to release and receive vital energy from higher unseen powers (*Works*, pp. 366–76). But does this unquestionable "vital value" furnish the evidence to verify the actual existence of those unseen, higher powers? Again, the "truth" question has surfaced, and in note 23 to page 401 James makes it clear what he means by it: "The word 'truth' is here taken to mean something additional to bare value for life, although the natural propensity of man is to believe that whatever has great value for life is thereby certified as true." John Smith[19] points to this note as "curious," for "on more than one occasion James gave the impression that 'value for life' is indeed his only criterion," whereas here, as in three earlier loci we have seen, he was obviously "looking for the 'something additional' which smacks of the very 'intellectualism' he repeatedly rejected in attacking rationalist opponents." The point is "important," Smith continues, "because it shows, first, that James was not in fact content with an appeal to 'value for life,' and, secondly, that he understood the inescapability of the question of truth or validity if there is to be a *philosophy* of religion in addition to the descriptive enterprise of phenomenology."

That this question of "truth" as "something additional" to value for life was in fact James's preoccupation in *Varieties* is clear, furthermore, not simply from this particular note, but also from the way he repeatedly postpones deciding on the question from page 263 to page 401; there, his phenomenological survey completed, he must face, at long last, the genuinely philosophical question. Granted, that a gamut of experiences persuades religious believers that an unseen world of higher powers has made contact with their higher selves, is this sufficient warrant for our holding it "true" that such a world of higher powers exists?

James answers by offering to furnish a "reconciling hypothesis" that may commend itself to both scientists and religionists. But "Who says 'hypothesis' renounces the ambition to be coercive in his arguments." The most he can do is "offer something that may fit the facts so easily that your scientific logic will find no plausible pretext for vetoing your impulse to welcome it as true" (*Works*, p. 402). A modest truth-claim, surely, and James expresses it candidly enough. But that closing phrase, referring to our *not* "vetoing [our] impulse to welcome it as true," turns out, on examination, to be simply one more variant expression for his "will to believe," and one more implicit admission that genuine verification of the theistic hypothesis is beyond our human reach.

In *Pragmatism* James remains entirely consistent with

that carefully limited stand. Referring to *Varieties of Religious Experience*, he assures his hearers that his "book on man's religious experience" has, "on the whole been regarded as making for the reality of God": "making for," but not quite verifying. But this may be due to the limits of our experience: and James expresses his firm belief that our human experience is not "the highest form of experience in the universe"; our relation to the "whole universe," he is convinced, is much the same as our household pets' relation to the "whole of human life." And so "we may well believe, on the proofs that religious experience affords, that higher powers exist and are at work to save the world. . . ."

But will the religious hypothesis which pragmatic philosophy offers prove to "work better in the long run"? The question of pragmatic verification of theism has been squarely posed, and, significantly, James refuses to give any "dogmatic answer" to it; "The various over-beliefs of men, their several faith-ventures, are in fact what are needed to bring the evidence in." And James has once again fallen back, it would appear, on his familiar "judgment day" verification—but now, with the implication that that answer is no real answer, after all.

A Pluralistic Universe conveys essentially the same message: the "drift of all the evidence" he has surveyed in his earlier lectures seems to him to "sweep us very strongly towards the belief in some form of superhuman life with which we may, unknown to ourselves, be coconscious." This observation again recalls his familiar analogy comparing us humans to the dogs and cats in our libraries, observing all the phenomena of our human lives, yet "having no inkling of the meaning of it all." The facts of psychology, pathology, psychical research, and religious experience "establish, when taken together, a decidedly *formidable* probability in favor of" the view he has been arguing for, even if some details must remain vague and problematic (*Works*, p. 141). And this final lecture ends (*Works*, p. 148), as we have already seen, on a note consistent with all that has gone before: by presenting the "faith-ladder" which James has already encouraged us to equate with his earlier "will to believe."

James's "Appendix" in *Some Problems of Philosophy*, on "Faith and the Right to Believe" (*Works*, pp. 111–17), features that same "faith-ladder" once again. He has already told us (*Works*, p. 112) that the "evidence" for the kind of universe he is arguing for requires a certain (precursive) "good-will for its reception," and added, in words strongly reminiscent of "The Will to Believe," that there are instances where we "*cannot* wait" upon further evidence, but "must act, somehow; so we act on the most *probable* hypothesis, trusting that the event may prove us wise." Once again he reminds his adversaries—whom now he calls the "intellectualists"—that "not to act on one belief, is often equivalent to acting as if the opposite belief were true," so inaction would not always be as "passive" as the intellectualists assume. It is one attitude of will, or, in his older coinage, one "passional" decision competing against the passional decision he is commending; it "is itself an act of faith of the most arbitrary kind" (*Works*, p. 113). The character of the world's results, he concludes, "may" depend in part upon our acts, which "may" depend in turn on our "religion." So "faith . . . remains as one of the inalienable birth-rights of our mind" and "*may* be regarded as a formative factor in the universe, *if* we be integral parts thereof, and co-determinants, by our behavior, of what its total character *may* be." The once-confident "M + x" argument has, alas, here died the death of a million qualifications.

In the closing part of that Appendix, on the "pluralistic or melioristic" universe, James seems to be straining toward a more positive affirmation. But he begins cautiously, in a hypothetical vein: "if the 'melioristic' universe were really *here*, it would require the active good-will of all of us . . . to bring it to a prosperous issue." The very next sentence shifts abruptly into the indicative, but the reader is clearly meant to understand those indicatives as still qualified by the "if" he began with: "It will succeed just in proportion as more of these [independent powers which constitute it] work for its success. . . . If each does its best, it will not fail." James now shifts back into the hypothetical mood: the destiny of this melioristic world "hangs on an *if*, or on a lot of *ifs*—which amounts to saying . . . that, the world being unfinished, its total character can be expressed only by *hypothetical* and not by *categorical* propositions."

But here the neuralgic question once again arises: if a sufficient number of us act on our belief, can we make the world *so much* a better place as to provide verification for our theistic and melioristic faith? It would seem not, for "we must recognize that even though we do *our* best, the other factors also will have a voice in the result. If they refuse to conspire, our good-will and labor may be thrown away." Nothing can "save us from the risks we run in being part of such a world." "'*If* we do our best, *and* the other powers do *their* best, the world will be perfected. . . .'" "[T]his proposition," he concludes, "*expresses no actual fact, but only the complexion of a fact thought of as eventually possible*" (emphasis added).

But now comes a surprising affirmation: "We can *create* the conclusion," by which James means the "perfected world" toward which his meliorist theory points. Again, though, that sudden indicative should be understood in consistency with what immediately follows: we "can and may, as it were, jump with both feet off the ground into or towards a world *of which we trust the other parts to meet our jump*" (emphasis added). "*Only so* can the *making* of a perfected world of the pluralistic pattern ever take place."

Clearly, then, James meant all the indicatives that dot this summary to be qualified by the "if" contained in his very first sentence. Religious conviction remains what it was in *A Pluralistic Universe* and in the works that preceded it: the best hypothesis James can propose. Its standing may have improved, its credibility been enhanced in the meantime, but it remains an hypothesis nonetheless. Faith, as in his earlier formulation, still "runs before evidence" and requires that we bring to our survey of the evidence a precursive "good-will, our 'will to believe.'" Despite its more cautious title, the thought and expression of this Appendix on the "right" to believe turns out to be remarkably continuous with that of "The Will to Believe." Or, in slightly different terms, even when defending our "right to believe," James is brought round, at the crucial step in his argument, to validate the "will" to believe.

And however much one might wish that the contrary were true, the mature William James never assured his readers that their theistic faith could be pragmatically verified by their experience within the span of their lifetimes.

NOTES

1. See Patrick K. Dooley's review in *Transactions of the Charles S. Peirce Society*, 21 (1985), 569–76; having first reduced the claim of precursive influence to an affirmation that "passional demands tremendously influence our beliefs and over-beliefs," he then dismisses it: "this is surely no news." But a survey of recent defenses of James's essay will show that if this be truly old news, the word has not quite gotten around— indeed, Dooley himself does not seem to be fully aware of its implications. See, for example, Saul Smilansky's summary of the scholarly situation in "Did James Deceive Himself About Free Will," in ibid., 28 (1992).

2. See his *Pragmatism as Humanism: The Philosophy of William James* (Chicago: Nelson-Hall, 1974), pp. 62, 68, 87, 107, 113; that this control is rooted in the "structures of human nature," see pp. 48, 68.

3. (Cambridge: Harvard University Press, 1979), pp. xi– xxxviii. All citations of James's works are from this series, and citations from his "popular lectures," including "The Will to Believe," are from this volume (abbreviated to WB). For evidence that these vacillations did not alternate between a "will" and a "right" to believe, as one prevailing view would have it, see James C. S. Wernham, *James's Will-to-Believe Doctrine: A Heretical View* (Montreal: McGill-Queens University Press,

1987), pp. 11–16. Since Wernham does not take the precursive influence of the passional explicitly into account, I have serious difficulties about his more positive disposition of this whole question.

4. See the examples of this language below.

5. I refer to the well-known adage that no one is held to do the impossible, hence if a course of action is morally obligatory, it must also be naturally within the powers of the agent so obliged.

6. See above, pp. 107–22.

7. For these repeated allusions to Kennedy's suggestion, see above, p. 20 and note 1 to that page, where I warn the reader that I will later have some refinements to make on his proposal; then pp. 67, 69n4, and finally 84 where I make it clear that I had grave difficulties with Kennedy's proposal as a blanket solution to the problems raised by James's essay. Dooley's truncated quotation from my page 116 excises precisely those qualifying terms which specify that *if* one considers the "friendship" metaphor as the *only* normative metaphor James gives to illustrate the process of belief, Kennedy would *appear* to be right.

8. See above, p. 116.

9. See his review of the first edition of this volume in *International Philosophical Quarterly*, 26 (1986), 189–91, at 190.

10. McDermott approvingly quotes my argument claiming that "no one can 'will' a friendship, but 'no friendship was ever joined without some willingness to believe.'" But he infers that I thereby "acknowledge[d] that James later changed the 'will' to believe to the 'right' or 'readiness' to believe." First off, I "acknowledged" no such thing about James; but, second, I would now distinguish between "making friends" and "keeping a friendship": see my remarks below.

11. This attitude of belief would have something provisional about it, granted; humans being what they are, we must never trust even our finest friends as though they were perfect.

12. See note 3, above.

13. In his review in *Theological Studies*, 46 (1985), 755, Terrence W. Tilley observes that the "courage" to believe I conclude to be James's essential message cannot alone "indicate which of the many strenuous ways we should walk in our pluralistic universe," and that I should "draw this out more clearly." Tilley is asking me to take on a task which James

himself postponed, and I think wisely. To borrow a distinction from John Smith, "The Will to Believe" and its companion pieces lay down the lines of "approach," whereas only in his later works, like *The Varieties of Religious Experience,* does James address himself to a second, and quite distinct task, that of identifying more specifically the "substance" of religious belief. Unless we get clear on the fundamental *attitude* required for any and all forms of personal theism (the precise form of "religious belief" to which James's thesis applies: WB 31–32), whatever be the closer specifics of its object—unless we are prepared to accept that religious belief as such requires that we embrace the "strenuous mood"—it would be idle to move on to the more specific question of "which of the many strenuous ways we should walk." In his earlier essays, James is keenly aware that he has his hands full just persuading his scientific-minded hearers to take seriously their human obligation to shake off their agnostic inertia and *walk.* Later, he feels he may shoulder the onus of indicating *which way* they should do their walking. But that "second step" would be entirely futile unless the need, indeed the obligation, for taking the first step were firmly assured.

14. See Ralph Barton Perry, *The Thought and Character of William James,* 2 vols. (Boston: Little, Brown, 1935), II, 354; and Henry Samuel Levinson, *The Religious Investigations of William James* (Chapel Hill: University of North Carolina Press, 1981), p. 277.

15. See especially the classic chapter on "Habit" in *The Principles of Psychology.*

16. James quotes the Latin and attributes this tag to Cicero at WB 77. In his 1875 review of Wundt, printed in *Works* XVII, p. 297, he unpacks the expression as applying to that "generous divination, and that superiority in virtue which was thought by Cicero to give a man the best insight into nature. . . ." This, I am convinced, implies a more carefully discriminated view than the Darwinian "pre-established harmony" Gerald E. Myers attributes to him in *William James: His Life and Thought* (New Haven and London: Yale University Press, 1986), p. 280.

17. See above, Appendix B.

18. See above, p. 192.

19. John E. Smith, *Purpose and Thought: The Meaning of Pragmatism* (New Haven: Yale University Press, 1978), p. 164.

Index